HOUSE CALLS
STARTUP MANUAL

HOW TO RUN A LOW-OVERHEAD, HIGH-PROFIT PRACTICE

...and get your life back.

DR. CHRISTOPHER SEGLER
DOC ON THE RUN

Publisher: Virchow Press
www.virchowpress.com
Cover design: PixelDroidDesigns
www.facebook.com/ixeldroidstudio
Back cover photo credit: Jock McDonald

This publication is designed to provide accurate and authoritative information in regard to the subject matter covered. The author and publisher make no warranty or guarantee as to the accuracy of the information herein. It is sold with the understanding that the publisher is not engaged in rendering legal, accounting, or other professional services. If legal advice or other expert assistance is required, the services of a competent professional advisor should be sought.

Library of Congress Cataloging-in-Publication Data

Segler,Christopher P., 1968 –
House calls startup manual: how to run a low-overhead, high-profit practice
and get your life back.

ISBN-13: 978-0-9965226-1-8 (hardcover)
ISBN-10: 0996522611

ISBN-13: 978-0-9965226-0-1 (paperback)
ISBB-10: 0996522603

ISBN-13: 978-0-9965226-2-5 (ebook)
ISBN-10: 099652262X

1.   Business 2. Medicine 3. How-to

Printed in the United States of America.

First Edition

My son Alex was five years old when I decided this book needed to be written. He was seven when it was complete. I dedicate this to him, because he played patiently and quietly while I wrote, understanding that this book would give you more time with your loved ones, too.

Table of Contents

Introduction:
Life Before and After House Calls

One of the pivotal moments in my career occurred (not surprisingly) a few months after the birth of my son, Alex. I had a brand-new office that was 3,600 square feet. I had seven employees, including a physical therapist who worked under my direction in the office. I was swamped with patients. By any outward measurement, I had a successful practice.

But the reality was that I spent several hours before I went into the office and several hours after that workin\\g on patient-related matters. I generally spent all day on Saturday at the office signing charts. I worked on a computer at home most of the day on Sunday, as well.

One Saturday morning, my wife said that she wanted to go to lunch with her friends. "No problem!" I said. " I'll just take Alex with me to work. The office is brand-new, anyway, so I don't mind letting him crawl around on the floor. I can always put him in the baby backpack, as well. You can just stop by the office after you have lunch and hang out with your friends and pick him up and take him back home."

Later that afternoon, my wife took a picture that changed my life. There, through the window-to-ceiling glass of the front of my office, I stood signing charts. I was perfectly positioned at my counters, which were custom built to my specifications so I wouldn't have to stoop over. I had realized after many years of standing at counters that, as someone who is 6'2" tall, I have to bend over a standard-height counter. So mine were all custom built to the exact height I wanted.

And in that picture, there I stood, at my custom-built counter height, signing charts with my infant son, Alex, slumped over, sleeping uncomfortably in a backpack while I worked. When I saw that image, I felt sick to my stomach. Somehow, it not what I had envisioned when thinking about spending time with my son. This was not exactly "quality time."

Today, when I spend time with Alex, I am fully present. I turn off my cell phone. I look him in the eye. I am not preoccupied with email. I listen to him when he is trying to explain something to me. I play with him. I enjoy our time together. In the mornings, I get up and fix breakfast for my son. We practice writing letters of the alphabet. If we have time, we might even do something creative like make a paper toy monster together. The point is that we spend time together before he goes to school.

In the afternoons when I pick Alex up from school, I am usually the first parent to arrive. I have his bicycle in my trunk. We go to Lake Merced or Ocean Beach so that he can practice riding his bicycle. We eat dinner together. I read him a bedtime story.

All of these interactions were impossible before I changed my practice.

Chapter 1:
Advantages of a House-Calls-Based Podiatry Practice

There are many advantages of a house-calls-based podiatry practice. Here are a few:

Extremely low overhead

In fact, when compared to a conventional podiatry practice, there is almost no overhead. There is no rent to pay. There are no employees to pay.

Absolute freedom and flexibility in scheduling

This is perfect for people who like to spend time with their children, exercise, or volunteer.

I once had lunch with another doctor who asked me, "Do you really answer your telephone when you are running?" I explained that I do. He asked, "Doesn't it bother you that you have to answer your phone to talk to patients when you're out for a run?"

I replied, "I guess it depends on your perspective. If I told myself that it was annoying that I had to talk to patients when I was out running, maybe it would. But instead what I do is tell myself that if I were working at Kaiser or in some other conventional practice model, I wouldn't be out for a long run at three o'clock in the afternoon."

Immediate payment

With a house-calls-based practice, you are not required to take insurance, because you are not competing with all the other podiatrists in your area. Because you do not accept insurance, you get paid immediately. Immediate payment is much better than net 30, 60, or 90 days—or, worse yet, never.

If you're reading this and you have been in practice, you understand the pain of providing care for services provided and then never receiving payment from the insurance company. It happens to everyone. It is the reality of accepting insurance. In five years of providing house calls with a cash-based practice, I have never had an episode where I didn't get paid.

Lower malpractice insurance

Malpractice insurance carriers offer part-time insurance rates for those who do not have full-time practices. This is not based on the number of hours that you work but on face-to-face time with patients. I currently see about one ninth the number of patients I used to see in a conventional practice. My malpractice insurance is based on one-quarter time. I also pay about one fourth the standard malpractice rate for the same level of malpractice protection.

The best office in the world

I routinely post pictures that I take while I'm out on house calls. The majority of the podiatry offices I have been in are dark, enclosed boxes. Many of them are in the basement. Even those that are relatively nice cannot hold a candle to the views that I see when I'm out treating patients.

Variation in routine

I like variety. I like the idea of driving around town and going to different settings all day long. It probably doesn't hurt that I am in one of the most beautiful cities in the world. However, if I were in any other city in America, I still would prefer making house calls as opposed to sitting in a dark, claustrophobic office. I like the variation of seeing different parts of town all day.

Increased job satisfaction

There is no question that a house-calls-based practice model allows me to use the full knowledge that I have acquired through years of school and clinical practice. I get to interact with patients in a meaningful way. I get to apply everything that I have learned.

This simply was not true of a conventional practice. When I had a practice that accepted insurance in an office setting, I had treatment protocols that were applied to the most common conditions. I had a large staff that was trained to take over many of the functions that I as a physician would provide. Patient education was provided by protocol by the staff.

I now perform all physician functions myself. These range from taking the full history, to making a diagnosis, to providing patient education and explaining the treatment plans. I feel like a real doctor again. I used to feel like an assembly-line worker. I am able to stop and think about what is really going on with a complicated patient. I don't just offer them one treatment and then tell them to come back in a week or two.

The patient and I talk about "if this ... then that." We talk about all sorts of scenarios that could unfold based upon how their treatment is evolving. We talk about different recovery scenarios. We talk about options. All of this is what I initially perceived would be my job when I decided that I wanted to be a doctor. Today my practice is exactly as I want it to be. I share my expertise with patients, and they get better.

Gratitude from patients

Although I only see about one ninth the number of patients I used to see, I receive about ten times as many thank-you letters. Believe it or not, I actually receive tips. I have had patients who pay more money than I asked for. I had one surgical patient pay me $100 extra in cash on the day of his surgery just so I would "do an extra-good job." No insurance company ever offered to add a gratuity. For that matter, no insurance company ever sent me a thank-you letter, either. Although it is not my primary goal, it is nice to feel appreciated. The money is not bad, either.

Higher income

If you have a practice the grosses $500,000 per year, it sounds like you're making a lot of money. If your expenses happen to be $400,000 per year, you're not making a great living at all. In fact, you're making less than does the average podiatrist in the United States.

If you have a house-calls-based practice and you earn $250,000 per year, with almost no overhead at all, you're making significantly more money. After all, the goal of work is to earn money to facilitate the lifestyle that you choose.

Time for friends, family, and other interests

When you have a house-calls-based-practice with significantly lower overhead and immediate payment for services provided, you have a lot more freedom. If you don't want to work on the weekend, you can charge more to work on the weekend. If you don't want to see patients in the evening, you either can choose not to see those patients, or you can see them at a much higher rate. By earning significantly more money during these more lucrative windows of opportunity, you have the freedom to spend time with your family or pursue other interests.

A side benefit that many don't consider is that, when you have a practice with multiple employees, high rent, and other expenses, you are probably less likely to take a vacation, simply because you know it will cost you thousands of dollars. When I go on vacation now, I no longer worry about paying seven employees to sit in the office on Facebook while no income is being generated. In fact, I often schedule remote consultations while I'm on vacation so that I can continue to generate income and follow up with patients, even while I'm sitting by the pool in Hawaii. That's not a joke. I actually have performed remote consultations while on vacation in Hawaii while my son played in the swimming pool.

When I had a conventional practice, I took very few vacations, and all were based around podiatry conferences. Last year, I went to Houston twice to visit my sister, I trained for and competed in an Ironman race, I went to Portugal, I went to Los Angeles, I went to Las Vegas, I went to Washington DC, and I went to Hawaii—twice.

This year, I'm training for and competing in a marathon and four Ironman races. I also will visit my brother in Phoenix twice. I'll visit my sister in Houston twice. I'll spend one week on the French Riviera and another week in Italy. I'll spend two weeks in Hawaii. I'll go to Miami to visit friends. I'll vacation in Mexico for a week, as well. I'll go to Las Vegas. I'll go to Los Angeles a couple times to visit friends. This amount of time away from work would have been unthinkable with the limitations of a conventional practice.

Chapter 2:
Myths and Realities of a House-Calls-Based Podiatry Practice

Myth	Reality
You need lots of wealthy clients. When I first started a house-calls-based podiatry practice, I thought that I would have only two possible types of clients. The first would be elderly people who were too frail to travel and found it too much trouble to get out of the house to see a podiatrist. I (wrongly) believed this would constitute the bulk of my practice. On the other end of the spectrum, I thought I would have clients who were extremely wealthy and willing to pay top dollar for the convenience of house calls.	I have found that the two groups of people that I thought would make up the bulk of my practice are the minority. In fact, the majority of patients I see are patients whom I find interesting. They are young, well-educated professionals who are athletic. They recognize the limits of the current healthcare system. They want more personalized interaction. What they perceive they are getting from me is real expertise with full explanations. They don't want rushed medicine, and they're willing to pay for it.
You'll spend all your time cutting	I cut very few toenails. I'd bet that, in one week in my former conventional practice, I cut more toenails than I did last year in my house-calls-based practice.
You have to offer low prices. Initially, when I started a house-calls-based practice, I thought I would need to offer low prices to compete with other podiatrists in the area. San Francisco is known to be one of the most saturated markets in the country in terms of podiatry services.	What I have found is that I have created a niche market that has no competition whatsoever. As a result, I can charge much higher prices than I ever thought possible.
You have to work long hours. When I started a house-calls-based practice, I really thought that, to make a good living, I would have to work long hours to make up for the low prices that I was going to charge. Of course, I figured that this would be a good trade-off, given that I would have low overhead. I knew that I could still make a great living, but I thought that I would have to work hard. Although I have never had an aversion to hard work, I have decided that hard work is vastly overrated.	It is remarkable how few hours I work in order to earn more money than I did in a conventional insurance-based practice. Getting paid significantly higher fees with no delay in payment, coupled with a fraction of the overhead, makes for a much more comfortable lifestyle.

Chapter 3:
How to Market Your House-Calls-Based Practice

Attracting patients

First of all, I don't recommend "finding" patients the way conventional practices do. It is far preferable to let the patients find you. Attraction is much more effective than promotion.

The key is knowing your target market. Search for "Achilles tendinitis Madison, WI" and see what comes up.

Fill the empty spaces where profitable patients exist. Offer whatever no one else offers.

There's a saying that goes, "It takes no more effort to dream a big dream than it does to dream a small dream." By that same token, it takes no more effort to acquire a profitable patient than it does to acquire an unprofitable patient—so why not focus on the profitable ones?

When I had a conventional practice, I marketed several different ways:

- I advertised in the Yellow Pages. I had a large ad in the Yellow Pages that cost well over $1,000 per month.
- I had a full-sized billboard advertisement for over $1,000 per month.
- I took out ads in local papers.
- I sponsored (paid) local sporting events.
- I hosted luncheons or breakfast meetings at primary-care-physician offices, rheumatology

offices, and endocrinologist offices. I bought lunch or breakfast for the entire staff of the office to arrange these meetings. I hoped that they referred their foot/ankle patients to me. I usually did this once a week. The cost of these events ranged from $50 to as much as $200. It also took a few hours out of my morning.

Today, I do exactly zero marketing of this kind. Yes, I do some marketing—just not conventional marketing.

I do not have a Yellow Pages ad. In fact, I am not listed in the Yellow Pages at all. For that matter, I'm not even listed in the White Pages of the telephone book. I don't want patients to find me if they rely on a phone book. These patients are not in my target demographic.

I do not buy lunch for anyone at a medical office.

I do not buy cookies to feed the gatekeepers at medical offices of any type.

"Today's view from the office"

As you already may have encountered in your discussions about starting a house-calls-based practice, many of your friends, family, and colleagues will think you're crazy. They might even scoff at your idea, or tell you there's no way that it will work. I, too, had my sanity questioned when I decided to switch from a conventional practice to a direct-pay model. But after my first year of success, I found myself wanting to point out to my skeptical colleagues that not only was my practice working, it also was quite enjoyable.

I had a misguided idea one day, which turned into what may be one of the most effective marketing tools I ever stumbled upon. I was out driving around San Francisco making house calls. I was sitting in a patient's home in the Marina, and we were talking. She was sitting on a couch in front of a huge picture window. As we talked about her foot pain, I found myself gazing past her shoulder and looking out at the absolutely stunning view of the Golden Gate Bridge, San Francisco Bay, and Alcatraz. When our visit was completed I asked her, "Would you mind if I take a picture of your view?"

"Of course not!" she replied.

I took a picture of the view with my phone. I then uploaded it to Facebook with the caption "Today's View from the Podiatry Office."

I openly admit that part of my motivation was to jab at my naysaying podiatry colleagues who I knew at that moment were slaving away in their windowless podiatry dungeons. But what happened was something remarkable. After routinely posting these sorts of pictures, I started to get inquiries from new patients who were friends on Facebook.

Many of these friends were people whom I had met through my local running club or triathlon club. Some of them were people I probably wouldn't be able to recognize unless I met them at a social gathering and they happened to have a printed copy of their Facebook profile pinned to their shirt. Yet they knew about me, they knew that I did sports-medicine house calls, and they knew that I would service their area.

The cost of acquiring these new patients through this form of marketing cost me exactly zero dollars.

Using the changes in healthcare policy to create a niche

Question: How has Obamacare affected your concierge

practice? *Answer:* Quite well, thank you.

Part of the key to building a successful cash-based practice is that you have to offer something that's not currently being offered by other doctors. People will not pay you for the same care when they can get it for free.

The current trend in healthcare delivery, of course, is to leverage the physician's time by utilizing lesser-trained associates. This used to mean nurse practitioners or medical assistants. However, now this currently is extended to the associates known as "HSG," or high school graduates.

Here was my experience in seeing a standard physician one time: I was asked to explain the multiple entries of my medical history with the office staff, and the physician didn't even read it the report.

Chapter 4:

Nuts and Bolts of House Calls

To run a successful house-calls-based practice, you need only a few things:

- Your expertise
- A way for patients to reach you
- A system for scheduling patients
- A simple medical-records system
- A system for getting paid
- Office equipment
- Essential house-call/clinical supplies

We will talk about each of these.

Your expertise

If you are reading this, you likely have been in practice for some time—certainly long enough that you have become tired of the conventional practice system. The problem isn't that you are confused about how to treat patients. The problem is that you don't like your current practice model. So you already have all of the clinical skill and expertise you need to succeed.

A way for patients to reach you

The vast majority of patients who call me found me online. All you really need is a website, and a free Yelp! listing. I built all of my websites myself. Most of them cost only $100 or so to get up and running. If you choose, you can spend more money and have a site professionally built. The website is critical, but it doesn't have to expensive. With a website and a cell phone, you have everything you need to connect with patients.

A system for scheduling patients

Any calendar system can be used to schedule patients. I have used a variety of methods. For years, I bought an old-school bound planner every December. I would hand write every note from prospective patients and write the appointments in the calendar. This method is simple and effective. However, there is the obvious huge risk of losing the calendar. Frankly, this was my biggest worry. I had heartburn over the idea that the calendar could be lost or stolen.

I currently use a digital calendar backed up online. You can use free ones such as iCal or Google Calendar. Just check with your legal counsel to make sure that you are HIPPA compliant. With an online calendar, you will never lose it. However, you must make sure that your appointments get saved consistently.

There are paid online scheduling software systems, as well. Skedge.me is an online appointment system that I have used for the past few years. The advantage is that some (but not many) patients prefer to schedule an appointment online as soon as they decide they want a house call. For this reason alone, it is worth having the online-scheduling option available.

The downside is that patients schedule based on their preference alone. If they call you to schedule, then you may have the option of scheduling them at a time when you already have another patient on the calendar who is close by, as opposed to being across town. Coordinating appointments geographically can save large blocks of time.

I do not love Skedge.me. The system has some bugs, and patients have complained about a range of issues. I will keep using an electronic calendar supplemented with a patient-directed online scheduling mechanism, just likely a different software system. Fell free to email me to see if I have found a better system and switched yet.

A simple medical-records system

When I am at home, I wear a corded headset plugged into my cell phone. When the phone rings, I answer it, "Doc on the Run—this is Dr. Segler."

I begin taking notes on the front page of a blank New Patient Encounter form. I record the person's name, chief complaint, and any portion of the subjective section (NLDOCAT) that is volunteered. By the time they finish explaining why they are calling, I have recorded the majority of the Subjective portion of what will become their clinical note.

Once they ask for an appointment time, I record the demographics on the front page of the New Patient Encounter form (name, address, phone number, and email address).

I send a confirmation email to the patient with attached Medical History and HIPPA forms. If the patient is elderly, I also attach a Medicare Opt-Out Agreement. The patient will print these at home, fill them out, and hand them to me on the day of the visit. These completed forms comprise the past medical history, social history, family history, review of systems, and so on. I will place them in the patient's file.

I then create a file using a manilla one-third tab file folder. I write the patient's name on the tab with a red Sharpie. This file eventually will hold all of the patient's clinical record.

I also create a New Patient Folder. This consists of the a description of the practice ("About Our Practice" sheet), letterhead with the patient's name and date of visit written on it, and any patient-education information that may relate to the suspected condition I will be treating.

During the actual house call, I take notes, draw illustrations, and list the diagnosis and plan on the letterhead in the New Patient Folder. I take a photo of the completed clinical notes for the patient that I wrote on the letterhead. I then can print this and place it in the patient's chart, thus completing the "Assessment" and "Plan" sections of the note for the visit. If the patient calls me later to ask a question, I also have this copy of the notes they are looking at, and about which are asking for clarification. The Patient Chart is stored in a locked file cabinet. As a back-up, I also scan the chart into PDF format that can be stored on multiple drives to be HIPPA compliant and guard against possible loss of the medical record. Having a backup is good.

A system for getting paid

Getting paid is important. As doctors, we are not used to getting paid. But you need to get used to asking to get paid and expect to get paid for everything you do, right when you do it. Part of this practice model is *payment at the time of service*.

The confirmation email I send to patients explains this:

> The cost of a new patient house call appointment and new patient consultation is $300. Certain treatments (such as custom orthotics, injections, surgery, etc.) require additional charges which, if necessary, will be discussed at the time of treatment.

> Payment for services is due at the time services are rendered. We accept check, cash, and all major credit cards. We will supply you with a complete Superbill (which contains all of the ICD-9 and CPT-codes your insurance carrier will need to process a claim and reimburse you for the visit.) Please be aware that we have opted out of Medicare, and our services cannot be billed to Medicare.

As soon as I finish treating the patient, explaining the condition, and concluding our discussion, I ask, "Would you like to use a check or credit card?"

Many times, the patients will ask, "Which form of payment is best for you?" I personally prefer checks. I can deposit them with my cell phone in less than one minute, and I have a clear record of payment to record on the patient invoice. Cash is fine, except I have to drive to the bank and stand in line to deposit it. Credit cards are convenient, but you pay for the convenience in two ways.

- **Fees.** I currently use Square to process credit-card payments. Square charges a fee of 2.75% of the transaction. If you manually key in the card number (instead of swiping the card), Square charges 3.5% + 15 cents.
- **Delayed deposit**. Square takes about 24 to 48 hours for the money to land in my account, depending upon the time of day of the initial transaction. Other merchant services are worse.

I use Square for all credit-card payments, and I love it. Square is straightforward and simple, and patients think it is cool that I can ring up their charge with my cell phone. It works flawlessly. The card reader is free, and there are no hidden fees, long-term contracts, or minimum charges. You can set up a list of items and charges that you frequently use such as House Call, New Patient Visit, Custom Orthotics, Fracture Walking Boot, Ingrown Toenail Removal, and so on. You can sign up and order a free card reader at www.SquareUP.com.

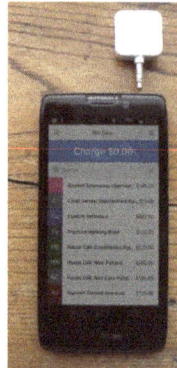

To use Square, you simply plug the reader into your headphone jack and swipe the card. The patent signs their name on the screen with a finger. The money gets deposited straight to your bank account.

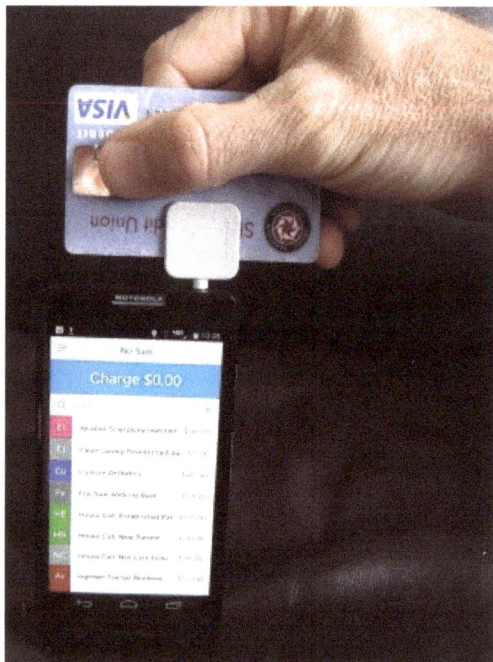

Whether you decide to get paid by check, cash, credit card, or PayPal, you must expect payment at the time of the visit. I *do not* bill patients and let them pay me later. If they want a visit or surgery financed, they can use a credit card. I am not a lending institution.

Office equipment

While you don't need much office equipment, there a few essential items: a cell phone, a computer, and an all-in-one printer, fax, and copier. In addition, I have an autoclave.

Cell phone

Although any phone would do, it seems somewhat unthinkable to see anything other than an iPhone or Android-based smartphone. If you are only planning to return calls, a standard cell phone will work—but the possibility of using a more technologically advanced phone to forward forms via email, accept credit cards, and use scheduling software seems like a much better option.

I personally use a smartphone. Specifically, I used to use a Motorola DroidX that I purchased in August of 2013. I used that smartphone for two years before upgrading to my current Droid Razor Maxx HD. The new one has a long battery life and takes great pictures for clinical notes. I have been using it ever since. I love it!

I am sure there are some newer smartphones, including the iPhone, that are faster and more user-friendly than this particular model. However, I don't particularly like spending my time learning new operating systems, and I can work very efficiently with this particular phone. I plan to continue to use it until it implodes.

Using a smartphone allows my cell phone to serve several functions. First and foremost, it is my appointment-scheduling center. Patients who call the office number listed on the website will reach me via this cell phone directly. I will speak to them and make a determination of whether I want to see them. If I do want to see them, I can schedule their appointment at the time that I first speak with them. They, of course, love this.

Secondly, my smartphone functions as my credit-card payment-processing terminal. As I mentioned earlier, I use a merchant account and credit-card payment-processing company called Square. By signing up for a merchant account, they send me a free credit-card reader that plugs into my smartphone. When a patient wants to make a payment via credit card, I simply swipe their credit card through the credit-card reader plugged into my smartphone. Their credit card is immediately charged for the visit. The program will even send an email confirming payment to the patient.

There are several reasons I chose this merchant-account credit-card-processing provider. I previously used a more conventional merchant account for processing credit cards but found that I was repeatedly charged for miscellaneous items such as a "batch header fee." Square has no hidden charges whatsoever. I am only billed 2.75% of credit-card charges. There are no additional charges. There are no minimum monthly charges. There is no contract. There is no fee if I decide not to use Square. There is no additional charge, even if I don't ever use the free Square credit-card reader!

The third function of the smartphone that is useful in payment processing is that I can take a picture of the front and back of any check that if patient has used to pay me for a visit and it will immediately deposit that check into my bank account. This now saves me the trouble of needing to drive to the bank to make deposits.

The fourth function of my smartphone that is useful in a house-calls-based practice is that also is a camera with excellent resolution. I use it to take pictures of the patient's feet, their shoes, their orthotics, their x-rays, and images that are relevant from their MRI or CT scan. When I get back to the office (i.e., home), I simply send these digital pictures wirelessly via bluetooth to my computer. I then can paste the digital images into the patient's clinical note for documentation and future reference.

The fifth important function of my smartphone is that I can use it as a handheld photocopier. When I write out written instructions or a prescription for a patient, I simply take a picture of those written instructions or prescription and then paste those into the patient's clinical note so that I have a permanent record of the information I have given them.

Computer

The computer is a necessary component of a house-calls-based practice so that I can schedule patients, send and receive email, create invoices, document clinical visits, and create the forms necessary to provide care to patients and document clinical encounters.

I currently use a laptop computer, but any computer will do. My current computer is a MacBook that I purchased six years ago. At the time I purchased it, it was the lowest-cost MacBook available. I since have upgraded the memory, and it has worked flawlessly for years. I have used the same computer to create patient-education videos, build websites, build all the forms necessary to run the practice, and carry out all day-to-day operations of patient care. The computer cost me less than $1,000. That means that I have spent only about $160 per year for the computer—and the depreciation, of course, is tax-deductible as a business expense.

All-in-one printer, fax, and copier

All of my desktop publishing is done with a low-cost all-in-one printer, fax, and copier. I currently use a Canon Pixma MX340. I'm not making this as a specific model recommendation, and it might be out of production by the time you read this. The point is that you can obtain a machine that will fulfill all of your desktop publishing, printing, photocopying, and faxing needs for roughly $100.

I use this printer to produce all of my patient-education materials, marketing materials, invoices, brochures, and letters. It is important to have the faxing function because faxes are much more secure than email. X-ray orders typically are faxed to imaging centers because it is fast and secure. In addition, the imaging facilities will fax x-ray, MRI ,and CT results back to me. The pathologist faxes the results in the same way.

Autoclave

I use a small autoclave to sterilize all instruments at home. Obviously, this is not equipment you will take with you on house calls. Although some physicians prefer to use cold sterilization techniques and save the expense of the autoclave, I feel that is worth the expense to have instruments that are sterilized with an autoclave. An autoclave can be purchased used in many cases through online auction sites such as eBay. Given this fact, it seemed inexcusable not to have one.

Essential house-call/clinical supplies

The house-calls mobile stockroom: a.k.a. "the trunk of my car"

Before you start thinking you need a box van to cart all of your podiatry supplies around the city on house calls, I should point out two important facts:

- I often ride a motorcycle to house-call appointments.
- The car I drive is a Mazda RX8. It has one of the smallest trunks of any vehicle on the planet.

No matter which of these two vehicles I choose, I can take everything that I need on a podiatry house call.

What you need for a podiatry house call

There are only a few "essential" items that I am compelled to take on a house call—and they all can fit in the trunk of my car.

Briefcase to carry new patient education information

The briefcase I carry on house calls contains essential items for educating the patient and processing payment. Here is what I always have in the briefcase:

- Business portfolio with business cards and letterhead for taking notes
- Patient-education materials on a wide range of topics to cover common conditions
- Custom orthotic samples to help patients understand what the device will look like
- Square card reader to process credit-card charges
- Anatomic foot model for patient-education discussion/demonstration
- Pads to offload lesions, metatarsal pads, aperture pads, crest pads, etc.
- Prescription pad (although I most often call prescriptions to save time for the patient)

Fracture walking boots and ankle braces

Fracture walking boots are essential pieces of equipment to be dispensed to patients who have stress fractures, severe cases of tendinitis, and severe sprains. I carry a selection of fracture boots (one each of small, medium, and large) in my car at all times. I dispense fracture walking boots to the patient at a charge of $125. Given that I currently pay about $40 for a fracture walking boot ordered from Gill Podiatry supply, these are profitable items, as well.

Most importantly, though, these are items the patients need to facilitate recovery. They also need these items immediately. It certainly is better for the patient if you can fit and dispense the fracture walking boot to them as soon as you treat them.

There also is the alternative of having a patient order a fracture walking boot online, if they need one. This is a reasonable option if you do not have a fracture walking boot available at the time your patient needs it. However, there always is a delay in shipping, and the patient may know not know how to fit themselves for the fracture walking boot correctly.

Orthotic casting materials

I have a single, small duffel bag, which is used to transport the orthotic casting materials. Inside of the duffel bag, I have two plastic bins that can be used to hold water for the casting process. After the patient has been casted, I pack the negative casts in the plastic bins to protect the casts from damage.

In the casting-materials duffel bag are:

- Roll of extra-fast-setting plaster
- 12 impervious (plastic-lined) towels
- Angle-finder level to measure calcaneal stance position
- Tractrograph to measure ankle and MPG range of motion
- Measuring tape to measure limb-length discrepancy
- Sharpie to mark lesions and/or prominences to be offloaded
- Bandage scissors to cut plaster
- 2 pairs of disposable non-sterile gloves
- Bubble wrap to pad and protect casts

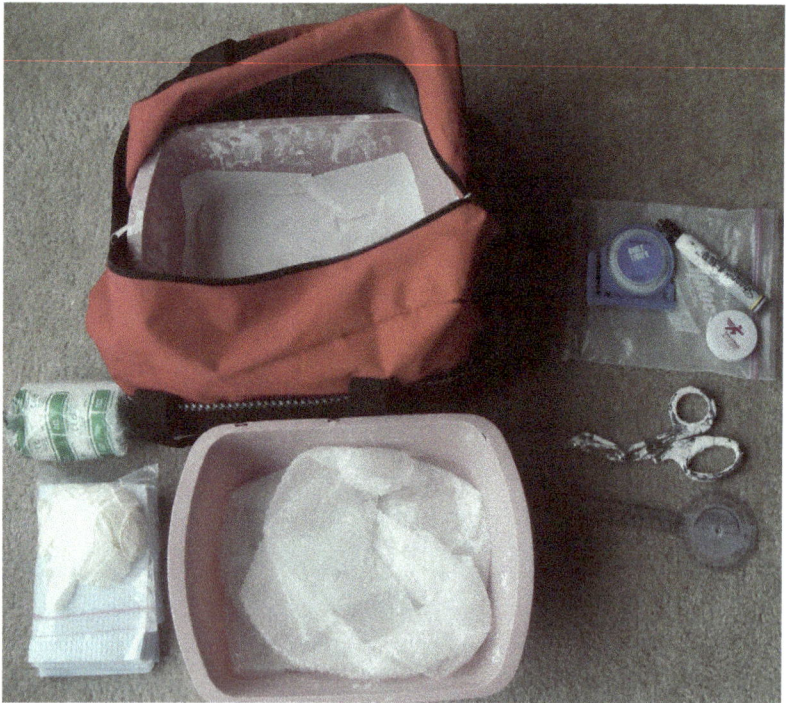

Mobile x-ray viewing box

Obviously, at some point, you will have to look at x-rays with the patient at home. It is best to have a clear viewing surface on which to view x-rays and point out abnormalities to the patient. Commercially available medical x-ray viewing boxes are heavy and extremely expensive. Instead, I use an Artograph Lightracer Light Box.

The Lightracer is an all-purpose art-and-craft light box for transferring designs and patterns. It works well for viewing x-rays. The translucent surface is illuminated by a fluorescent lamp. The 10" × 12" model comes with an 8W bulb and weighs just 3 lb. Lightracer plugs into any household standard 115V AC power outlet. It can be purchased online. At the time of this writing, it can be ordered from any online art supply retailer, and it is available from Dick Blick Art Supply (http://www.dickblick.com/products/artograph-lightracer-light-box/) for only $42.99.

Most physicians in conventional practices considering switching to house calls incorrectly believe that they need a mobile home, RV, or van to transport everything in the office to the patient's home. This is a fallacy. When you get a consult at the hospital, you certainly don't take the whole office with you. You decide what you will need and take only the most relevant items. There really are only a few considerations. When I go out to see a patient in their home, I need to be prepared to treat every possible condition that is profitable, probable, and/ or potentially litigious.

Four ways to determine what supplies you need

- Set up a "go to" supply drawer in your treatment room. Have your staff inventory what is used with each type of patient.
- Volunteer at a homeless clinic where you provide care for free and see what you use.
- "Trial by fire"—this is not recommended.
- Follow my list and then modify to fit your needs.

Your mobile-treatment-room cabinet

While I was in residency, one of my rotations had us working in a Department of Veterans Affairs hospital. In the podiatry department, all of the treatment rooms were the same. Each treatment room had a sink, a podiatry chair, a cabinet, and a rolling medical-supply cart with four drawers. Virtually everything that was needed to treat a patient was found within those four drawers. Not only were all the supplies within this one rolling cart, but it also typically contained enough supplies to treat a dozen or more patients. There were many unnecessary duplicates of bandages, except that it made it simpler for the nurses to stock the room.

I quickly realized that almost all of the supplies needed would fit into one drawer. If all of the supplies could fit into one drawer, they easily could be fitted into a well-compartmentalized case such as a fishing tackle box, which could be carried with me to any house call.

Many physicians think they need to bring an entire office with them when they travel to a patients home. Not true. I got to experiment with this during a long period of volunteering at a homeless clinic. I treated ulcers, ingrown toenails, and infections, removed foreign bodies, drained ganglions, and even did percutaneous hammertoe releases, right in a homeless shelter. This experience allowed me to begin to notice which supplies I really needed to provide care. The truth is that you can provide about 99% of needed care with carefully selected supplies organized in a simple fishing tackle box purchased at a sporting-goods store.

Treatment tackle box contents

(1) Coban 1" x 5-yard roll

(1) dexamethasone sodium phosphate 20 mg/5 mL (4mg/mL), 5mL vial

(1) betamethasone sodium phosphate/betamethasone acetate 30 mg/5 mL (6mg/mL), 5mL vial

(2) lotion samples: Gormel cream, 20% urea, Gormel aloe grand cream

(4) sterile tongue depressors

(4) sterile cotton-tipped applicator's

(1) sterile surgical skin marking pen

(3) povidone-iodine swab sticks, individually packaged

(4) packs of steri-strips, 0.125" x 3"

(4) 3 mL sterile syringe

(4) 6 mL sterile syringe

(1) 12 mL sterile syringe

(1) scalpel handle, sterilized

(1) penlight

(6) strips of parafilm to re-wrap/seal canthacur and phenol after use

(12) triple antibiotic ointment 0.9-gram individual packs

(1) tube betamethasone 0.05% ointment

(12) 1" x 3" Band-Aids

(6) 27-gauge sterile needles

(6) 18-gauge sterile needles

(12) alcohol prep pads, individual foil packs

(12) individual providone-iodine prep pads, individual foil packs

(1) phenol, small bottle (approximately 2 oz.), top wrapped with parafilm/placed in Ziplock bag (1) lidocaine hydrochloride jelly 2%, 30mL tube

(3) 1" x 75" conform, sterile, individually packaged

(1) iodosorb

(6) sealtex bandage strip, 0.75" x 1"
(1) tape measure
(12) individual measuring guides, single use with patient identifier area
(12) #15 blade scalpel blades, sterile, individually packed
(3) dry keratin specimen bag for pathology for nail specimens
(1) 10% formalin specimen pack for pathology for biopsy specimens
(3) tincture of benzoin, individual applicator packs (12 pair) non-sterile, latex-free gloves, size large
(2) icepacks, custom printed with practice name, phone number, website
(4) metatarsal pads, felt 0.25", adhesive backed
(6) 2" x 2" gauze pads, sterile, individually wrapped
(6) 3" x 3" gauze pads, sterile, individually wrapped
(1) ingrown toenail kit (see treatment protocol)
(12) plastic backed impervious paper towel drapes, 13" x 23"
(1) ethyl chloride topical anesthetic skin refrigerant
(1) Unna boot dressing, 4" x 10-yard roll
(1) sheet of felt aperture pads, precut, 1/16", for corns and hammer toes
(1) Coban, 3" x 55 yards
(1) 4" Kerlix gauze roll, sterile, individually wrapped
(1) 4" stockinette, precut to 30 inches in length
(1) Tensoplast, 2" roll
(1) 35 mL syringe
(1) 4% alcohol solution prepared with 0.5% Marcaine plain
(1) 2% lidocaine, 50 mL bottle
(1) Cordran tape, 4 mcg per square cm, 80" x 3" in length
(1) 2" silk tape
(1) 0.5% Marcaine plain, 50 mL bottle
(1) Canthacur-PS (7.5 mL bottle), top wrapped with parafilm/placed in ziplock bag
(1) 1% silver sulfadiazine cream 50 g jar
(1) Gentian violet topical solution 1%, 2 fluid ounce bottle
(1) EpiPen, epinephrine auto injector 0.3 mg
(1) reflex hammer
(1) blunt tipped bandage scissors, angled
(1) moleskin scissors
(1) foam padding, to modify, offload fracture boot
(1) adhesive backed felt, 0.25", one piece 6" x 12" to modify inserts or offload fracture boot
(1) container silver nitrate flexible caustic applicator sticks, sealed with parafilm
(2) Tensoplast, 1" x 5 yards, for taping pre-dislocation syndrome
(1) tuning fork: 128 Hz
(1) Dremel, lithium ion rechargeable model 1100
(1) Ruskin double action bone forces, sterilized, individually packed with curette and burr
(1) small nail nipper, sterilized, individually packed with curette and burr
(1) medium nail nipper, sterilized, individually packed with curette and burr

(1) large nail nipper, sterilized, individually packed with curette and burr

(1) tissue nipper, sterilized, individually packed

(1) sterile suture removal scissor, sterilized, individually packed with splinter forceps (1) sterile needle driver, sterilized, individually packed with forceps

(1) Ingrown toenail avulsion kit, sterilized (see ingrown toenail protocol for details)

Chapter 5:
Keys to Maximizing Revenue

To make a living, you don't need to be busy. You just need to get paid a fair rate for the time you spend providing care for your patients. You must decide how you will get paid and how much to charge for your services.

Insurance: To take it or *not* to take it, that is the question

Dr. G., a hand surgeon, is one the smartest people I have ever met. He is brilliant, comically irreverent, and insanely practical. He provided some of the most useful advice I have ever received during my residency training. But it had nothing to do with medicine or surgery.

One day, I had scrubbed in with him on several cases. As always, he reinforced basic surgical principles as we are working together. He also allowed me to do significant portions of the surgical procedure. At the end of the day, we were sitting in the dictation room. He asked me what my plans were for practice once I was done with residency. I explained that I planned to open my own private practice.

"Really! There aren't many people opening their own practices anymore," he said. I asked him if he had any particular advice. He turned around to look me squarely in the eye, and his face sort of lit up. "Yes, I do. Be very careful which insurance plans you agree to take," he said. "You cannot underestimate the importance of this. Now, listen to me, Chris—you probably will be tempted to accept every insurance plan under the sun, because you'll falsely believe that's the only way to build a successful practice. But you would be wrong about that." He continued, " Let me explain why."

He went on to explain that the city in which he practices has one of the highest HMO-saturation rates anywhere in the United States. Because of this, virtually every doctor in town accepts every single insurance plan that they are offered. Many of them believe that they are unsuccessful because they are unable to get their names on insurance panels that are "closed" to new providers. There is the perception that, since everyone has insurance and much of it is HMO type insurance, you cannot survive without accepting *all* insurance plans.

"This is B.S., and I can say that because I used to take all insurance plans," he explained. "One day, I realized that 50% of my hassles came from one particular IHC plan. So I explained to the partners in my group that I was no longer going to accept this insurance plan. They all said, 'You're crazy. That plan makes up about 25% of your business, and you won't survive if you don't see those patients.' But I knew I was right. So I stopped taking that plan. A few months later, I realized that most of my current hassles and lowest reimbursements then came from a particular United healthcare insurance plan. So I eliminated that one, as well. Again, my partners said 'You're crazy. That plan makes up about

25% of your business, and you won't survive if you don't see those patients.' But, again, I knew that I was right. And I canned that plan, as well."

He continued, "So, here's the best part, Chris: there are two hand surgeons in our orthopedic group, Dr. W. and me. Dr. W. also thought I was crazy when I stopped taking those two insurance plans. But you know what's happened? When I stopped accepting those two low-paying, high-hassle insurance plans, all of those low-paying patients had to go someplace else. They all went to see Dr. W. because Dr. W. still accepted the low-paying insurance plans. So his practice started to fill up with lower-paying, higher-hassle patients. But I don't have those people filling up my practice. Instead, the better-paying patients can get in to see me sooner than they would from other competing hand surgeons in the area. So I see all of these higher-paying-insurance patients instead.

"So here is the moral of the story. Today is 'Salsa Day.' Every Thursday, I get done with surgery early, and I head home, and my wife and I pick vegetables out of our garden, and we make fresh salsa. Without making very clear decisions on which insurance plans I would accept and which ones I would refuse, there would be no 'Salsa Day.'

"If you choose to do house calls and accept insurance, there is no question that you will be very busy. The question is, will you have the right kind of busy? Will there be any 'Salsa Day?' I doubt it.

"But if you don't accept insurance, and you do perform house calls, you'll be positioned to provide a remarkable value for the patients who are willing to pay for it. You'll be shocked at the range of patients who will pay for it. And, as a result, you'll have plenty of time for your own particular version of 'Salsa Day.'"

A couple of times a year, I make fresh salsa at home. I never do this without thinking of Dr. G.

Do you help your patients with submitting invoices to the insurance company?

This is one question I often get from doctors who are setting up house-calls practices. The short answer is, "No." If I wanted to serve as an intermediary between the patient and the insurance company, I would just accept insurance and bill the insurance company.

In terms of insurance claims, the only form I give to patients is the detailed paid invoice that has all of the ICD–9 codes and CPT codes. I do not give them any additional forms to help facilitate processing of the insurance claims. The reasons for this are simple:

- Certain insurance carriers may have specific forms.
- I do not in any way want to imply to the patients that I will assist in the process of making certain that they get paid by the insurance carrier.

If getting an insurance company to pay a claim were a simple, straightforward process, I still would accept insurance. I certainly do not want to become responsible for insurance-company denials. I actually have no idea how long it takes for patients to get reimbursed by insurance carriers, mainly because I have never asked. Yet this has never been an issue for me.

Can I keep Medicare as a backup, and just try to see young patients?

I think is a reasonable strategy to keep Medicare as a backup if you are really worried about this model working for you. The reality is that I see very few Medicare patients, anyway.

I would be hesitant to accept insurance and try to make up the difference with a mileage fee. You have to read your contract very carefully, and it is possible that insurance companies may prohibit you from accepting any additional fee other than the house-call fee. The other disadvantage of this, of course, is that you have to wait for payment and then follow up with the insurance companies to actually make sure that you get paid. Not having to worry about whether I get paid is what I consider to be one of the primary advantages of having a house-call-based practice.

When I accepted insurance, I had many many instances in which I provided care and never received payment from the insurance company, or was directed to try to attempt to collect from the patient because of some unforeseen deductible, coinsurance, or other issue. The statistical likelihood of collecting these fees later from the payment is dismal. In five years of running a fee-for-service practice, I've never had an incident where I did not get paid in full by the patient.

Who are the ideal patients, and what are the ideal conditions? And what can I charge?

To me the ideal patients and conditions are:

- Laser toenail fungus treatment
- Ingrown toenails
- Ankle sprains
- Peroneal tendinitis
- Achilles tendinitis (specifically Achilles tendinosis that needs PRP)
- Plantar plate injuries
- Ganglion cysts
- Orthotics patients (particularly those who need a functional pair and an additional pair for dress shoes or cycling shoes)
- Plantar warts
- Surgical patients including bunions, hallux rigidus, and plantar plate injuries

However, even when charging surgical fees of $1,600—$2,500, ankle sprains and ingrown toenails are significantly more profitable than surgery.

In terms of creating a fee schedule that won't scare off patients, you have several options.

When I first started doing house calls, I had fears that were similar to yours, and I only charged $125 for a house call. Within a short period of time, I increase my rates to $185 for a new patient and $125 for follow-up. After a couple of years, I increased my rates to $225 for a new patient and $185 for follow-up. At the end of 2013, I increased rates again to $250 for a new patient and $225 for follow-up. At the end of 2014, I increased rates again to $300 for a new patient and $250 for follow-up. With each price increase, I have encountered virtually no price resistance or decrease in the number of new patient appointments.

My goal is to have a *minimum* per-visit-value of $300. This in not difficult, given that an ingrown toenail typically means $425. An ankle sprain is usually $300—$510 (in one visit). I consider 15 patients in a week to be full. I can see more, but this is enough for me. Even at the low-end $300 per visit, *this still is over $200,00 per year.* And this is seeing only three patients per day at 10:00 a.m., 12:00 p.m., and 2:00 p.m. With this few patients needed for a successful practice, market size is less of a concern.

However, if you are really concerned about the fee schedule, you should realize that you have several options to offer discounts:

· You can waive the mileage fee.
· You can waive after-hours convenient-scheduling fees.
· You can waive weekend-scheduling fees.
· You can offer follow up by telephone or email free of charge.

If you waive *any fees* or offer *any discounts,* make it clear to the patient that you are providing these discounts. Whenever I do this, I actually specify and itemize any discounted or free services on the paid invoice to remind them that I have given them a discount.

Another option is to have a very low-cost price structure altogether. I have a friend who does house calls in a relatively economically depressed community. His business model is that he charges $50 for a house call. In fact, he charges $50 for anything—but he charges $50 for each and every thing. In that model, for a patient with an ingrown toenail, a house call is $50. Removal of the fibular edge of ingrown toenail is another $50. Removal of an additional ingrown toenail site (such as the tibial border of the same toenail) is an additional $50. The total equals $150. As another example, for a patient with thick toenails that need to be trimmed, a house call is $50. Trimming of thick dystrophic toenails is another $50. Trimming of painful calluses is an additional $50. The total equals $150. The vast majority of his patients are uninsured Hispanics. Most of them pay cash. According to him, they don't object to the up-sells.

You also can start with a lower rate for the basic house-call fee and then plan to up-sell the patient. A good example is a musculoskeletal condition such as an ankle sprain. I have attached an invoice that shows real charges to a real patient with an ankle sprain. This was a patient who wanted to maximize her chances of getting back to activity as quickly as possible. She had insurance but was paying for the visit herself, because she previously had been to an emergency/urgent care center where she was given the standard R.I.C.E. treatment that had little affect in terms of her ankle pain.

So, with this particular patient, if you were to see her at a relatively low-cost house-call rate, it still could become profitable if you simply offer to dispense items that she can use to speed her recovery. In this case, the total up-sell profit on these additional services was $225.33.

Ankle sprain items to dispense	Cost	Charge	Profit
Fracture walking boot	32.25	125.00	92.75
Darco web ankle brace	19.25	45.00	25.75
Ankle rehab balance board	11.00	29.00	18.00
Unna boot paste dressing	10.47	85.00	74.53
ACE wrap	1.23	10.00	8.77
Theraband	4.47	10.00	5.53
Total additional up-sell profit			225.33

PRP injections for Achilles tendinosis and chronic plantar fasciitis

For PRP (Platelet Rich Plasma) injections, I use the Biomet system. The representative gives me the centrifuge (on loan at no cost), which I take to the patient's home. At the same time I pick up the centrifuge, I also get the sterile kit to be used for the PRP injection. I pay $250 plus tax for the sterile kit.

Afterward, the procedure is simply to return the centrifuge to the representative. I generally just call the rep, and we coordinate as I'm driving back from a house call so that we literally just stop somewhere in between as we are crossing paths. It does not really take any extra time at all. This is a lucrative procedure, given that my cost is just over $250, and I charge about $1,300. This is actually better than most insurance companies' reimbursements for foot surgery procedures!

Laser treatment for toenail fungus

I normally charge $300 for a new patient house call, plus $850 for laser treatment. However, I often run discount specials on the website. The discount rate is $349 for all 10 toes. The entire procedure takes less than an hour. It is very low risk, and high profit. I use the Fox Podiatry Laser, a 1064nm wavelength YAG laser. It is small, battery powered, weighs about 4 lb., and fits in a metal briefcase that I can easily transport to house calls. Patients love that they can have the laser procedure at home.

Pre-paid care packages for routine care and wound care

I have not yet offered any specific wound-care packages, but I do offer prepaid routine foot care services for some patients. For example, I offer a "Nail Care Package" consisting of 12 in-home podiatry care visits at $120.83 per visit. It is inclusive of all routine, non-surgical services provided in the home. Weekend/holiday charges are not included. Patients must must pay for the 12 visits *in advance*, for a total of $1,450.00. This is a good option when your practice is starting because you get a more significant revenue stream upfront. It is appealing to patients because I normally charge $250 for each follow-up appointment. So the regular price is $3,000. The pre-paid discount is over $1,550 (more than 50%) off.

I certainly think it is possible to provide wound-care services at home, particularly for those patients who have difficulty getting out of the house. You simply need to consider the risk with any given patient. For this reason, I do not offer any of the prepaid packages until I have met a patient and determined that they will not be high risk or noncompliant.

Pricing strategies

There are many ways to choose sure prices and your fee structure. If your goal is to create a house-calls-based practice that facilitates a lifestyle that is actually enjoyable, you must choose your pricing structure carefully.

When I had a conventional practice, I accepted Medicare, Medicaid, and every insurance provider under the sun. One day, I had a large packet arrive from Big Insurance Group (BIG). I had an employee who had worked for nearly 30 years in the medical staff office at one of the local hospitals. One of her job functions was to review potential insurance contracts to determine whether or not I should accept the plan.

On this particular day, she opened the BIG package and saw that it contained a new insurance contract. She read through the insurance plan and then brought it to me with it adhesive arrows applied to every area of the contract that I needed to sign in order to agree to accept patients on this particular insurance plan.

For reasons I still don't understand, I decided to read the contract that day. Normally, I simply trusted Annie to make the decisions for me. When I read the contract, I realized that, by signing it, I would be obligated to accept *any fee* that the insurance company determined, once they actually developed their fee schedule, which they had not yet done and had not included, but to which I would agree, if I signed the contract.

I actually called my physician-relations representative at BIG. I asked her if this was a joke. She explained that I was a well-respected and prominent podiatrist within the community (shameless flattery). She went on to explain that BIG wanted to make sure that they had the very best doctor available on their panel and that I would be the exclusive provider for all the patients in this plan. She said that I would be flooded with new patients if I agreed to be the exclusive provider on this plan. She further explained that BIG had yet to determine what the exact fee schedule would be for patients on that plan.

I will admit that, at the time, being a young practitioner with many employees and rent to pay, the idea of being flooded with new patients was very appealing. But I'm not an idiot. I realized that, if I signed the contract, BIG would have license to pay me as little as they wanted for any evaluation and management code or procedure code. In fact, it would be foolish for them to pay me anything resembling a fair rate.

Fortunately, I had read an article about a similar fiasco that took place in New York and New Jersey where doctors unknowingly signed contracts that had no fee schedule provided, and which neither they nor their staffs had reviewed. In the end, they were obligated to see new patients for as little as $12 per visit. I could see 100 patients a day at this rate and still not make a profit.

Having talked to many doctors when setting up my conventional type practice, I realized that the most common way doctors choose to set a fee schedule is to pick a percentage of Medicare-allowable rates. This is one strategy, and I employed it when I had a conventional practice. When I think back to that time in my life, I realize that I often had episodes where I became resentful of patients. I didn't like diabetic patients who would stand in the shower, causing the stitches to come out. I didn't like to have to do additional wound care during the postoperative period for free just because a patient was irresponsible. I didn't like to pay my staff to stay late in order to see the patients who insisted they couldn't get there otherwise. I was afraid that they would sue me if I didn't see them on their own terms.

Today, I have set up my pricing schedule in such a way that I am never resentful of patients. I get reimbursed for what I perceive as patient convenience, and inconveniences to me. I have set my fee schedule to accommodate patients and make sure that, whenever I see a patient, I am always happy to do so. I just don't go see patients anymore where I think I'll be sitting in traffic for three hours and not getting paid for it. I charge extra for early-morning appointments, evening appointments, weekend appointments, and mileage.

But it seems foolish to me to choose to pick a fee schedule based upon persistently declining rates rather than what my time is actually worth. Today, my fee schedule is based upon three criteria:

• What I believe my time is worth
• How much I enjoy or dislike a particular procedure
• How convenient (or inconvenient) the encounter will be for me

Simply put, I don't really care how much Medicare pays for trimming dystrophic toenails. I don't particularly enjoy trimming dystrophic toenails. I charge accordingly.

As I am writing this today, a new patient who needs her toenails trimmed will pay $300 at the the time of service. A follow-up patient will pay $250 simply for trimming of toenails. I will not accept $38 (or whatever other current ridiculous fee Medicare pays), nor will I wait two or three months to see if they will actually pay me. I leave with a check in hand for the full amount. If I enjoyed cutting toenails, I probably would charge about half of what I currently do.

I apply the same logic for scheduling of appointment times. I don't particularly like to sit in traffic. As a result, I charge $95 extra if the patient wants to see me between the hours of 7:00 a.m. and 10:00 a.m. If the patient would like to see me after work, and I have to see them between the hours of 4:30 p.m. and 9:00 p.m., I charge $95 in addition to the standard house-call rate.

I also don't like to see patients on the weekend. But I will, for an additional fee of $195. This makes it very simple. If I see a patient on the weekend, those are two fewer patients I need to see during the week to earn the same amount of money.

When I first started seeing patients, I thought that I should create a fee schedule that was based upon what I thought was reasonable based upon mild knowledge of billing in a conventional practice. This is total hogwash. It is important to keep in mind that most patients receive an explanation of benefits that has a billed fee that is significantly higher than what most doctors ever expect to collect from an insurance company. Knowledgeable patients will use this higher figure as their reference point when considering the fees they will pay for medical care.

Although it is possible to be the lowest-cost provider in the area when performing house calls, that is a fool's errand. I do not want to compete with Walmart. No matter how hard I work, I believe it would be very difficult to win a price war when competing for the lowest-paying customer. That is just not a game I am interested in playing.

The process of sitting down and actually analyzing what you really think it is worth for you to perform a certain procedure is very difficult. I personally found that I was repeatedly trying to imagine what a patient would be willing to pay rather than what I felt I would be happy to receive as payment. These are two very different things—and it is essential to separate them in order to develop a fee schedule that you can live with, that will create the appropriate type of lifestyle for you, and allow you to cheerfully care for your patients.

Seven deadly sins of physician pricing

1. Creating fee schedules based on medicare rates
2. Believing your own ideas about what patients will pay
3. Selling on price
4. Comparing your prices to those of other service providers
5. Failing to differentiate your services
6. Failing to offer scaled convenience pricing
7. Pricing based on low self-esteem

1. Creating fee schedules based on medicare rates

I have attended many podiatry practice management seminars. I paid attention. I took notes. The bottom-line teachings of the practice-management seminars I attended encouraged podiatrists to increase income by increasing the number and frequency of better-paying procedures.

The profound advantage you have in setting up an insurance-free, house-calls-based-practice is that you are completely unfettered by seemingly arbitrary pricing set by someone else. You can charge whatever you want. Given these circumstances, if you are not charging enough for the procedures that you perform, you are solely to blame.

Because most insurance-company contracts are based upon a percentage of Medicare-allowable rates, there is a tendency to establish fees that are based in some relation upon Medicare fee schedules. Part of the reason for this tendency is that it seems simple to have a starting point. You take the numbers that Medicare has established as being "reasonable" and then make adjustments to arrive at rates you feel more comfortable with.

I personally believe that this is a mistake, simply because we know from sociology experiments that when you look at a particular price and you are told that that is the price, it has a profound affect on your thinking. It becomes very difficult to separate yourself mentally from that number and justify a significant increase. You are then forced to go through some extreme mental gyrations in order to believe that your services are worth more than what a cost-saving committee in Washington DC is attempting to force upon you.

In setting your own pricing schedule, it is better to look at every procedure you are likely to perform and simply determine what you think it is worth for you to perform that service. When you make that decision, you should look at the price discriminately and see if it would be profitable.

Another problem with establishing your rates in relation to Medicare-allowable rates is that, by definition, you are competing with Medicare providers. I believe that my practice has absolutely no relation to Medicare providers, because I don't accept Medicare. If the patient calls and asks about Medicare, I explain that I do not accept Medicare and have not for several years. I explain that, if they want care that is typical of someone who accepts Medicare-allowable rates, they should call a provider who does accept Medicare. I offer something different.

I don't promise better care—I just promise more-attentive, more-personalized, and more-convenient care. You will be surprised how many people, and across how many socioeconomic layers, are receptive to this idea.

There are very few people in the United States who at this point believe that our healthcare is in good shape. There are very few people who believe that they will receive the optimum healthcare delivered through the current system. They are tired of rushed visits, and they are tired of long waits. They are tired of having only a portion of their problems addressed in one visit.

You have to offer an alternative to this system, not just a slight variation on the current system. By explaining to patients that you are basically the same as a Medicare provider, they will get the impression that you are offering the same type of interactions. The most profitable fee schedule will be one completely free of Medicare influence.

2.   Believing your own ideas about what patients will pay

One of the simplest ways to free your mind of the self-esteem crushing the disease established by insurance companies and Medicare cost savers is to compare your perceived rates of reimbursement that are "reasonable" to those of other nonprofessional providers such as plumbers.

By simply setting your own house-call-fee schedule based upon what you think the market will bear and what you think people will pay, call three plumbers in your area and ask them how much it will cost to make a house call. Ask them about regular business hours, after hours, and weekends. Do you really believe that the average person is willing to pay a plumber to unclog a toilet but unwilling to pay the same amount to be able to walk pain-free? You have to carefully consider this question when setting your pricing.

3. Selling on price

Another basic tenet of podiatry practice management seminars is the idea that you can increase patient volume to such a height that you're able to generate a profit. It is possible to do this, but it requires high overhead. If you believe that this is the only path that is profitable, you should spend your time with the American Academy of Podiatry Practice Management and stop reading this book. They can teach you how to do this. I tried to do it and found that it was too stressful, so I found another way.

Make no mistake: I *do not* want to become a volume dealer.

The reality is that your patients don't want to be taken care of by somebody who views himself or herself as a volume dealer, either—so there is no reason for you to think about setting your prices low enough that you eventually will have a high volume of patients and the resultant profitability. On the contrary: you should set your prices high enough that you are profitable immediately. The higher the profit, the lower your stress, the more time you have to be attentive to details, and the higher the quality of care you will provide to your patients. This will produce more meaningful interactions for you and the patients, as well as increase referrals from raving patients.

4. Comparing your prices to those of other service providers

Another common mistake in pricing is to look at the other providers in your area and compete with them. Even if you are offering completely different services and a completely different level of service, you are competing with them if you are pricing in relation to them.

Let me be clear: I *do not* want to compete with anyone.

Competing with others for business just takes too much work. It makes no difference what the competitors in my area charge. They all charge about the same rates. They all take insurance. They all offer limited interactions, rushed service, and long waits. Some of them even offer extended evening and weekend hours. I know some of these podiatrists, and they seem to be some of the unhappiest people I know.

The goal in life is to be happy. Life is supposed to be fun, exciting, and blissful. Interactions with people (patients or otherwise) are supposed to be interesting and meaningful. In keeping with this, I believe it is best to set a fee schedule that facilitates a happy and successful lifestyle.

Most patients do not shop on price. Believe it or not, the vast majority of patients are not going to call three different providers and find out how much they charge for fracture walking boots. That doesn't mean that I charge more than anybody else for fracture walking boots—I just charge what I believe is going to be profitable.

My feeling is that if the patient is going to compare me to other practitioners in the area and is in fact shopping on price, I prefer that they go see another practitioner, anyway. The only patients I have ever had that are extremely difficult all mentioned price as a primary concern in our initial interaction.

This may lead you to believe that only rich people are going to pay cash for podiatry services. This also may imply that only wealthy people will refrain from considering price as a primary motivator of physician selection. This is all false. I have had college students, bartenders, manual laborers, and even the occasional billionaire, all of whom are equally happy to pay for convenience, increased attention, and a perceived higher level of care.

Every once in a while, I will get a call from a patient who attempts to negotiate lower prices by comparing my services to those of other providers. I use this argument to my advantage, highlighting the actual differences.

Real patient example #1

At 7:00 a.m. on a Saturday morning, I received a call from a patient who had a painful ingrown toenail. She had found my website online and noticed that I made house calls on Saturdays. She was located in Marin County just across the Golden Gate Bridge. At the moment she called, I coincidentally was putting on my cycling clothes and getting ready to head to Marin County to go for a six-hour bicycle ride.

The patient explained that she had an ingrown toenail that progressively had been getting worse over the past few days. She was worried that it might be getting infected. But even "more importantly," she had planned to go on a hike through the Marin Headlands later that day with her girlfriends, and she did not want to miss that experience.

I explained that, even though it was Saturday, I would be happy to see her. "I can certainly see you this morning," I said. "The cost of the new-patient house call is $300. There is an additional fee of $195 for appointments on Saturdays. If we can remove the portion of the ingrown toenail without injecting your toe to make it numb, there would be no additional charge. However, if we have to inject your toe to make it numb and do a small surgical procedure to remove the portion of the ingrown toenail, there would be an additional fee of $125."

"What?!" she exclaimed. "But I can see my normal podiatrist on Monday for a co-pay of only $40."

"Well, then why don't you call your 'normal podiatrist'?" I responded.

"Because he isn't open on Saturdays, and I don't want to miss this hike."

"I understand, but I don't accept insurance. And in much the same way that you don't want to skip your hike today, you certainly wouldn't believe that it is reasonable for me to skip my bicycle ride in order to fix your ingrown toenail on an emergency basis on a Saturday—for only $40," I replied.

"Okay, that makes sense. How soon could you see me?"

"Well, if you don't mind me showing up in cycling clothes, I can be there in about 20 minutes."

"Great. I will see you then!" she exclaimed.

Real patient example #2

One afternoon, I received a call from a woman who explained that her mother was homebound and needed to have her toenails trimmed. She further explained it was very difficult to get her mother in and out of the house, and she often had to hire a service to carry her down the front steps, put her in the medical transport van, and then carry her back up the steps after her doctor appointments. The entire ordeal always would wear her mother out.
I explained that I would be happy to see her mother to trim her toenails, and that my rate for a house call was $300.

"What?!" she exclaimed. "$300! But when my mom goes to Kaiser, they trim her toenails for only $40."

"Wow!" I answered, "The podiatrist from Kaiser comes to your house for only $40?"

Well, no, of course not. We have to pay someone to transport my mother to the doctor's office at Kaiser in order to do get her toenails trimmed."

"I see. Then we are talking about something very different. Instead of paying someone to transport your mother back and forth to Kaiser, and exhaust her in the process, I could come to your home and trim her toenails for her. In fact, I could see her tomorrow at 2:00 p.m., if it's convenient. If you instead prefer to take her to Kaiser, I certainly understand that," I replied.

She said, "Okay. That sounds great. We will see tomorrow at 2:00 p.m."

Both of the patients mentioned in the examples above scheduled appointments at my rates. Keep in mind that both of these patients initially implied that they were accustomed to paying one fifth to one tenth of the rates that they ended up paying. One even posted a rave review on Yelp!

Use any attempt at comparing your services to other providers as an opportunity to explain the extraordinary advantages of convenience that you offer.

5. Failing to differentiate your services

I don't offer the same services as every other podiatrist in the area. I offer something different, and I make this clear when I answer the phone. When my cell phone rings, I answer with, "Doc On The Run—this is Dr. Segler."

There is often a pause followed by, "You mean this is actually the doctor?"

"Well, yes, didn't you call a doctor?"

"Um, yeah, but I didn't think I would actually get to speak to the doctor!"

"Who came up with that rule?" I ask. "We believe that if you are calling to talk to a doctor, you should get to speak to a doctor. If you need help right away, you should get help right away. We also believe that you ought to be allowed to get your questions answered whenever you need them answered."

The patient immediately knows that they're going to get something different.

I believe it is best to fill empty spaces. It is best to offer services that others are not. Direct physician response, accessibility, attentive expertise, and convenient medical care are all conspicuously lacking in virtually every community across the United States. If you are offering these enhancements to your patients, if you are offering slightly better service, you are offering something entirely different. It should be priced accordingly.

When I see a patient at home, I typically will spend an hour or more with them. I read their x-ray films, MRI, and/or CT scan with them in their home. I explain their condition in great detail. We discuss their marathon and triathlon training programs. We discuss their shoes. I look at their over-the-counter orthotics and discuss what is good and bad. We consider their short-term and long-term goals. We come up with strategies for injury prevention in the future.

Patients are quick to acknowledge this difference. Here are some actual comments posted on-line by patients:

> He spent two hours at my place going over the MRI, all my symptoms, and x-rays. I have never seen a doctor for more than a few minutes in my life. Anyway — he diagnosed a partial rupture and prescribed the proper care. I think he is hands down the best doctor I have come across, and I highly recommend him if you are having a problem that does not go away. It would even be worth the airfare to SF.

— Heidi L., Los Angeles

Dr. Segler is pretty awesome. He came by to the house in San Mateo from the city pretty quickly, as I had an emergency which needed to be treated right away. Let's just say this was something that's very painful in my big toe. He was only supposed to be with me for an hour but was there longer because that is what was needed. He was very caring, very friendly, and very professional all at the same time. I've never had an experience with a doctor as warm as Dr. Segler is. He was just very pleasant to be around and explained in great detail what was the issue. He talks a bit, sure, but I much rather have much more information than not enough information. I will also, in the near future, go to him for a new treatment for treating my partially ruptured Achilles.

— Calvin L., San Mateo

Dr. Segler is an excellent doctor for athletes with foot and ankle problems, for several reasons:

1)As an athlete, he has empathy for the time and effort investment of training and fitness, and places value on retaining fitness as much as possible. He will work with you to help you keep your fitness while fixing or recovering from your injury.
2)He is exceptional in that he spends as much time with you analyzing and discussing your problem as you need. I have never before had the opportunity to discuss an ailment for 1.5 hours with a medical doctor. After that amount of time and intellectual effort, I feel confident that I understand the nature and extent of my injury, and what I need to do to resolve it.
3)His house call business model is also unique, and can simplify the logistics of finding a suitable appointment time and location.

Note that with all these strong qualities, he can afford to not accept/process insurance claims, but his pricing is competitive and he is worth every penny. He provides timely invoices by which one can submit insurance claims oneself.

— Dr. M., Livermore

He spent over an hour with me answering questions; explaining the anatomy of my foot with drawings, props and x-rays; and helping me understand what I can do to help my own cause. When was the last time a doctor spent an hour with you? Let alone made a house call? And it was next day service at a very reasonable cost. Have a foot issue? Call Doc on the Run. No question.

— Andy L., San Francisco

I echo the strong endorsements of the other reviewers.

I have had chronic but intermittent pain on the tops of my feet (one foot in particular) for about two years. This flared up more a few months ago when I was training on steep terrain for a strenuous multi-day hike. I saw a podiatrist about this twice — he didn't give me any useful info, wanted me to have an MRI done at his firm's facility 25 miles from here, and mentioned possible surgery before I even took my socks off! I didn't want to go down that path, so didn't have an MRI done and was wringing my hands about what to do. As I procrastinated, the incidents of pain were coming more frequently and at those times the pain was more pronounced.

I contacted Doc on the Run on the recommendation of a top-notch sports manual therapist and was very pleased with the resulting service. Dr. Segler got back to me right away and accommodated my schedule. He is professional, knowledgeable, and warm and inspired my trust. He spent about an hour and a half at my home — listened to my history, reviewed an x-ray taken a few months ago, examined my foot, drew diagrams of the feet for me, gave me some materials relevant to my issues, gave me a diagnosis, and told me lots of things to do and avoid doing to help my foot heal. His fees are very reasonable.

His is an interesting business model for delivering medical services. I was very pleased.

— Marrianne, Atherton

I've been living with PTTD for about a year and felt like I was running out of options. There is no magic bullet, but it was so nice to hear concisely what all of my options are. He is the fourth doctor I've seen for this problem and by far the most thorough and well versed. His drawings and models of the foot went a long way for me to wrap my head around the problem.

Lastly the cost is very reasonable. I've easily paid twice as much for a small fraction of the information that I received. If I have one regret, it's that I didn't find him a year ago.

— Joshua M., Thailand

Dr. Segler's knowledge of sports issues and treatments is expert and formidable. He is compassionate, patient and available to a degree that is completely unique. He is professional, yet warm and down-to-earth. Never brisk, impatient, condescending or elusive, Dr. Segler answers every question carefully and takes time and interest in educating his patient. He offers a perspective that only a doctor who is himself an endurance athlete can possess. His rates are very reasonable. With quick availability, he comes to your home and takes the time needed to do a careful history, analysis and treatment plan. He's waded through various bureaucracies on my behalf in order to get important tests done correctly. Dr. Segler is a true advocate, whose first priority is getting the job done for his patient. He is available directly by phone or email, with prompt response — hours or even minutes. How unusual is that? Amazing!

If you're an athlete of any type (or non-athlete, for that matter), dealing with a foot or ankle issue — you've found you're Doc, hands down. Dr. Segler is one of a kind!

— Erik C., Albany, CA

I had no time all week to go to a podiatrist near where I work in Menlo Park — so I decided to give him a ring for a house call on Saturday. I was wary using a guy that does house calls. I asked myself, could this be legit?

BOY was I surprised. Dr. Segler is one of the best doctors I've been to (generally speaking), and the whole house call thing was amazing. I was on my own couch on my iPad the entire time he was fixing my toe. It was truly such an amazing experience, wow.

— Dave S., San Francisco, CA

Dr. Segler is quite simply fantastic. He came to my house. Imagine that? We sat together and he explained how and why my foot was hurting. (I'd taken his x-ray order and shared the results of an MRI with him days before our appointment.)

Unlike another sports med podiatrist I'd consulted, he left me with several alternatives for coping with my problem. He listened to everything I said, responded in ways that let me know he actually heard me and shared a little of his own experience with exercise, pain and healing.

He also encouraged me to email him with questions or just to let him know how I was doing. Best of all, his suggested treatment is yielding results so far. And, when I emailed him, he answered me promptly.

What could be better than working with a doctor whose humanity is palpable and whose knowledge and skill are extraordinary? Oh, and he comes to your house: no driving, no parking, no waiting room, no receptionist, just Dr. Segler himself.

Vina W., Stanford, CA

Thanks to a REAL Doc for a wonderful visit. I highly recommend him. Best visit I've had with a doctor in many years. He actually spent time listening to my version of what I felt was wrong. He sent me for x-rays prior to visit. Showed them to me and explained my problems in great detail. For a diabetic with foot problems that was a tremendous visit. I now understand what I need to do to correct my problem!! That is MAJOR for a person like me who wants to continue walking on daily basis and prevent foot ulcers. I loved the explanations, the drawn illustrations and his in-depth instructions on how to best solve my problems. Thank you for a wonderful visit, Doc. I also loved the fact that he came to me and I had no long wait in an office. What a joy to meet a Doc with a great personality and obviously a very caring person. Money very well spent and worth more than the charge ... now you never find that today!! Appreciate your honesty also Doc. You are way cool!!

— Barbara C., Menlo Park, CA

I unfortunately ruptured (snapped) my Achilles tendon while snowboarding this winter. At first I was hoping it wasn't that bad, but after doing a little web search soon realized it was either a partial or full rupture and needed some medical attention stat. I called Dr. Segler and explained what had happened and explained I thought I had some sort of rupture. I wound up making an appointment. What was cool was that he had me go to a local place to get a MRI before my appointment with him, as he would need the MRI to diagnose the condition properly. Cool because it saved me time and an unnecessary initial appointment and money as I was confident I had some sort of serious rupture. It turned out it was a full rupture and I was in surgery in two days (quick is crucial for this surgery if possible).

Surgery went well and I am well on my way to getting my mojo back. I've got nothing but good things to say about my experience with Dr. S. and think he's an athlete's ace. Trying to not make this too long I'll surmise and just say he is knowledgeable, informative (drawings and all), professional, progressive, a good listener, an excellent surgeon, and he makes house calls! My experience with Dr. Segler has been truly top notch and I highly recommend the good Doc.

— **Richard I., San Francisco, C**A

Dr Segler went above and beyond making three trips to get my orthotics just right and customize them to my feet for maximum comfort. Beyond just orthotics the guy has sound medical knowledge and, this is the best part, knows how to listen. I've seen 6-9 doctors since my accident and Dr Segler was the best listener. As a result, I got x-rays that we discussed and discovered I still have a "boney block" in my right ankle. I am going to have a small procedure to fix the block and give me more range of motion in my right leg. This should be the last of my procedures (for now) and I think this will get me back to 100 percent — Dr Segler is a huge part of my recent comfort with his orthotics and he helped me find out what else was wrong with me so I can treat the issue and get back to 100 percent. Thanks Dr Segler. Oh and he makes house calls?? Who makes house calls these days?? Dr Segler does! So easy. I also got my orthotics covered by insurance and Dr S gave me all the paperwork to make it easy breezy.

— **P.W., San Francisco, CA**

Dr. Segler is beyond great! I have been suffering from a plantar's wart that I had attempted to be removed twice by another podiatrist. Dr. Segler came to my house with everything that he could possibly need, walked me through the issues and all possible treatments, and treated me. He even calls in the prescription for you to your pharmacy! How much better does it get? No traveling to an office, no waiting, no rush and distraction, and no waiting at the pharmacy. It was so nice to talk to him about other issues and questions without feeling rushed. I found him to be extremely knowledgable, patient, and one who enjoys his work. It was refreshing to have a quality doctor visit by someone who loves what they do. I only wish other practitioners had similar services/ options.

— **Marrianne D., San Francisco, CA**

I was finally recommended to Dr. Segler by my primary care physician and was extremely satisfied with our first appointment. He drove to my house, which is located in the somewhat remote town of Montara, and charged me a very reasonable fee for a highly comprehensive exam. I finally have a legitimate diagnosis and prognosis for my ankle and have already noticed a significant improvement in balance, flexibility, and performance after only one week of using Dr. Segler's tailored physical therapy plan. Dr. Segler is not only a highly experienced and accomplished foot & ankle specialist but also a caring, competent professional who offers a wide array of non-surgical alternatives. He has the skill set and creativity to save you thousands or even tens of thousands of dollars in unnecessary surgical, post-surgical, and physical therapy bills. I wish I had access to a professional of his caliber for every healthcare modality.

— Viajero P., Montara, CA

Podiatry house-call pearl: *You should read these reviews because they are all real patients explaining why they feel that paying for care was worth every penny. You should structure your services in a way that will elicit similar reviews in your house-calls-based practice. In most cases, it is not the expertise, but the perception that a doctor has finally taken the time to help them understand themselves and their condition.*

6. Failing to offer scaled convenience pricing

This concept is not new. If you book an economy rental car, you are not going to expect that you will get a full-sized Cadillac, a Lexus, or a convertible sports car for the same rate. People expect to pay more for comfort, convenience, and perceived enhancements.

Even at the bottom of the pricing spectrum, consumers expect to pay for increased convenience. Southwest Airlines is the leading low-priced air carrier. Choose the cheapest flight and get where you need to go for the lowest rate. Pay roughly 190% of the cheap fare and you get flexibility in the form of refundable airfare and no charges for same-day flight changes, if you decide to fly at a different time on the same day.

Pay 200% of the cheap fare and you get the added flexibility of priority boarding, including a fast pass through security so that you don't have to wait in line.

Same flight. Slightly more convenient. Costs twice as much. People are used to this tiered system of pricing.

7. Pricing based on low self-esteem

Before you skip this section, you should realize that this is an insidious factor that affects us all. I am not trying to suggest that you need to get up in the morning and do personal affirmations in the mirror like Stuart Smalley, but you need to be wary of the factors that can force you to drop your prices at the urging of patients you don't want to see in the first place.

As I am writing this, I dodged one of these bullets last week. The patient scheduled an appointment via my online scheduling software for a Saturday afternoon. The comment section explained that the appointment was for her 92-year-old mother. She wanted to be clear about price. She wanted to make sure that there would be no additional fee above the $300 house-call rate as specified on the website and in the confirmation sent to her via email when she scheduled the appointment (pricing red flag #1).

I sent a reply to the patient by e-mail explaining: "The cost of a new-patient house-call appointment and new-patient consultation is $300. Certain treatments (such as custom orthotics, injections, surgery, etc.) require additional charges which, if necessary, will be discussed at the time of treatment. There is no additional charge for trimming of thick toenails or calluses. I am not certain if you realize, but you have requested a weekend appointment. There is an additional weekend charge of $195. Please let me know if this is your preference."

The woman replied and explained that she has a very busy work schedule and "can't afford" (pricing red flag #2) to take time off of work, but that she wanted to be there for the initial appointment for her mother. She continued in that same email, "How much would future appointments for nail trimming be? I don't want to start this unless we can follow through" (pricing red flag #3).

Here is the point when my fatal error began. I started to fear that I was going to lose the patient. Keep in mind that this is somewhat ludicrous given that the patient was actually north of San Francisco, and I don't like to trim toenails, anyway. And I already had agreed to see the patient without charging my usual mileage fee (pricing error #1). And yet, I started to become concerned that I was going to "miss out" on this income. So I felt pressured to offer the following concessions: "The last standard-rate appointment is from 2:00-3:30 p.m. I could likely do a later appointment to accommodate your schedule. With some flexibility, we could potentially see you at 4:00 or 5:00 p.m. and waive the after-hours fee in addition to waiving the mileage fee, so there would be no additional charge." (This of course now makes this potential visit a double-whammy of pricing error #1). "Follow-up visits are $250, and there is no additional fee for trimming of toenails."

In that paragraph, I simultaneously made three mistakes:

- I set up the expectation that, if they desired, I would see the patient after hours with no additional fee.
- I set the expectation that I would travel beyond my usual range without any additional fee.
- I set the expectation that, with a little urging, I would lower my prices at will.

The patient of course replied with an email saying that it would be great if I could see her for the initial appointment, and at regular monthly intervals, at 5:00 p.m. If I were to accept this, I would commit to spending approximately two hours in traffic, plus caring for the patient, for

$250 every month until the patient died. I never would be able to raise the rates beyond this for this particular patient, because I already had created an unreasonable set of expectations. And it was *entirely my fault.*

Fortunately, my scheduling software came to the rescue by sending an appointment confirmation for her Saturday appointment, which was still in the system. This completely unintentional accident frightened the patient into canceling. She sent a frantic email saying that she could not afford the additional fees for the weekend appointment and wanted to make sure that the appointment was canceled. I replied to her immediately and said that it was absolutely no problem and we had cancelled her appointment altogether. I wished her the best of luck. I received a cordial response in return. Bullet dodged; lesson learned.

Podiatry house-call pearl: *Be the pricing police in your own practice. You have to create your fee schedule based on what works with your lifestyle (not the penny-pinching patient). When a prospective patient asks you to deviate from your fee schedule, you need to hold those boundaries. Just say no. You will get other calls.*

The right kind of "busy"

I often get questions from other doctors about how to begin a house-calls practice. Many physicians are intrigued by this idea. The thought of low overhead and immediate payment seems to be appealing. But by far the most frequent question I hear is, "How busy are you?"

It is an interesting question. It is interesting to me primarily because I paid very close attention to the parameters that resident physicians and students used to determine whether or not a physician or surgeon is actually perceived as being successful. It all boils down to "how busy" the doc is.

When I was a resident, I was very busy. I was assigned to specific rotations. I had clinical responsibilities. I had surgical responsibilities. I was also the chief resident, which meant that I had additional teaching and educational responsibilities. I also worked on multiple research projects, which meant I had a wealth of tedious administrative responsibilities. I was much busier than most other residents.

But I made no more money than any other resident. If you think "busy" is a reasonable measure of success, you should read that sentence again. I was much busier than all of my colleagues—and I made no more money—for being "busy."

The current cost-saving measures with Medicare in the nationwide saturation of health maintenance organizations have forced doctors to become "busy," but being busy does not assure success. A better measure of success to me is how much money I make. A better measure of success is how many hours I must work in order to earn a six-figure income. A better measure of success is determining how much money I get paid to see each patient.

Let's compare two different types of work on a Saturday. If I were busy rounding on diabetic postoperative inpatients in the hospital, I would have a hard time feeling that this was success. In essence, due to the "global periods" associated with surgical procedures, inpatient rounds are not billable. This, of course, is in spite of the fact that rounding on patients in the hospital seems to take much longer than in pretty much any other setting. I don't get paid to look for the chart. I don't get paid to find the patient who may be off getting tests someplace. I don't get paid answering questions for the nurses. This is not income. This is not work for which I am paid. This is all free work.

Instead, let's imagine that I received calls on a Saturday morning from three different patients, all of whom had ingrown toenails that needed to be removed. Assuming that they all wanted them removed immediately, I would be busy for about half of the day. But this is a very different kind of "busy." At this writing, I charge $300 for a house call. I charge $125 for partial toenail avulsion. I charge an additional $195 to do a house call on the weekend. This is $620 per patient. That is $1,860 in only a few hours.

Compare that rate of reimbursement with the treatment of a severe diabetic foot infection. In only a few hours of treating ingrown toenails on the weekend, I would get paid more than I would for the initial workup and evaluation of a diabetic foot infection, the first surgery which most often would be a surgical procedure consisting of an incision and drainage to remove all of the purulence. There would be no reimbursement for daily trips to the hospital in order to conduct rounds while awaiting for the infection to clear, and no reimbursement for taking phone calls to answer questions regarding orders. I would be reimbursed for the second definitive surgical procedure to close the wound. However, I would be committed to postoperative follow-up for a period of 90 days without any further reimbursement, unless the patient had returned to the operating room. In my experience, the postoperative care would involve daily rounds at the hospital for three to five days after the first surgery and two to three days after the second surgery. They then would be seen (provided everything was going well) on post-op days #7, #14, #21, #28, #42, and #84. That is approximately 14 visits, many of them in the hospital, all for significantly less reimbursement than taking care of a few ingrown toenails on the weekend. Diabetic patients with infections that lead to partial foot amputations are also significantly more likely to sue you. This is definitely the worst kind of busy.

Today, I have very clear financial measures of the right kind of busy. Each month, I decide exactly how much money I intend to make. At the end of the month, when I tally the amount of income, if it matches the number that I wrote down as a goal, I call that the right kind of busy.

I also have emotional measures of the right kind of busy. Some of these are easy to quantify. If I take at least six vacations per year, that is the right kind of busy. If I pick up my four-year-old son from daycare one to two hours earlier than necessary at least three days per week so that I can take him to ride his bicycle, play at the park, or otherwise spend viable time with him, I call this the right kind of busy. If I run or ride my bicycle when the sun is high in the sky five days per week, I suspect I am engaging in the right kind of busy.

If I get too many calls from patients, have too many patients scheduled, and my stress level rises, I start to realize that I must have too much of the wrong kind of busy. Every time this happens, I make adjustments in my fees and the types of patients I agree to see. I, of course, eliminate the lowest-paying (most time-consuming), most stressful patients. So every time I feel stress creeping into my life, I make changes to facilitate every other area of my life. As a result, I consistently see fewer patients, while simultaneously watching my income creep upward. This is the only way to ensure more of the right kind of busy.

Even with a poorly run, loosely developed fee structure in a house-calls-based practice, it is feasible to earn an equal or greater income seeing approximately one ninth of the patients seen in a standard practice. This is feasible working less than half the time.

This is the best kind of busy.

Chapter 6:
Saving Time Is Saving Money

How to recognize efficient patients

If you set up your practice correctly, you should only attract patients who fall into your particular demographic and have a particular mindset. Busy professionals are best. Part of the reason that I find busy, professional, young, active patients to be the best patients is that they don't like their time wasted. As a side benefit, they will not waste your time, either. They may want the full explanation, and this desire will facilitate meaningful patient/physician interactions while allowing you to enjoy sharing the full knowledge that you've acquired over the years.

Professionals generally conduct themselves with the same rules of personal performance and personal interaction that they do in their business. They have a very specific agenda. If you listen to these patients, they will help you determine their needs. Some of them may even outline the main goals and expectations of the house call in an email sent to you before the visit.

How to spot a time vampire

When you first start your house-calls-based practice, you will be excited and thrilled when patients call. Any time you hear the cell phone ring, you are almost assured that you will have some immediate income. This is indeed wonderful.

However, the time will come when it becomes difficult to answer the phone because you have too many patients. In my own experience, I have determined that having too many patients often will mean that I have many wonderful, friendly, profitable patients and only a few of the wrong types of patients.

By eliminating the few patients who are causing the most headaches, that feeling of being too busy simply doesn't occur. To eliminate them, I must be able recognize them. By eliminating the 20% of patients who cause the 80% of time expenditure and headaches, your life will improve significantly. You will sleep better, you will enjoy your time with patients better—and, yes, you will make much more money. This is not complicated math.

The problem is that it might be very difficult to recognize when you already have taken on too many of these difficult patients. My measure for this is simple. If I feel like I am stressed out on a Friday afternoon and think I will need to work on patient notes over the weekend when I normally would be riding my bicycle or spending time with my son, it's time for me to look at my patients and see who needs to go.

Unreasonable and/or ambiguous patients

In the past year or so, I have spent a great deal of time focusing on this aspect of practice management. The process has been transformational. It has gotten to the point that, when the phone rings and I speak to a patient, I usually can tell within the first 30 to 45 seconds whether this will be one of my patients. Believe it or not, I also have gotten to the point that I sometimes can tell if the patient is going to be enjoyable, profitable, and appropriate for my house-calls-based practice, even if I don't answer the telephone.

A patient who has absolutely no idea what they need or what they want is unlikely to be respectful of your time. For this reason, I have found that the most time-consuming patients don't like to leave messages. They are unsure of what they are trying to get from you. Because of this, they cannot leave a clear explanation of their problem or a clear explanation of their expectations of you in a voicemail.

These are the patients who repeatedly will call you, hang up, and not leave a message. They call and hang up over and over instead of leaving a voicemail. The reason for this is not that they are trying to be rude but that they simply are trying to get you on the phone so they can talk to you and sort out their own thoughts while they're having a conversation with you.

How to pick an unprofitable patient out of a line-up

One morning, I was about to participate in a 10K race. I was standing amongst the crowd of runners talking to my friend James. James is an attorney. We were talking about good clients versus bad clients, profitable clients versus unprofitable clients. James said something to me that I will never forget:

"You can make a whole lot of money just not seeing certain people."

The questions are, how do you identify those certain people? How do you pick out the ones that you don't want to see? What do you do with them when you identify them?

The obvious answer to these questions is that you should avoid selling based on price. You should not try to attract patients who are going to perceive they are getting the best-price, lowest-cost treatment option. You must sell based on something other than price.

There is one podiatrist in my area who advertises "$100 off custom orthotics." Whenever a patient calls me and starts to ask questions about price, I quickly tell them that I am not the cheapest guy in town. If they ask me for a specific recommendation on who provides low-cost treatments, I recommend them to this particular podiatrist. They often ask me if this podiatrist will do the exact same thing that I do. I explain, "Probably not. In fact, I don't even know exactly what she does. All I know is that she advertises that she offers discounts In her podiatry practice. So if you're looking for a discount, this is probably the person you should call."

Whenever a new patient calls, I try to identify the phrases that I have noticed are commonly used among patients that are difficult, unprofitable, and time-consuming. Interestingly, this triad seems to occur. The people who want the lowest cost also seem to demand the most time. It is a strange paradigm that I don't exactly understand. But I don't need to understand all the workings of electricity to know that, if I flip the light switch, the light bulb will turn on.

Ten key phrases unprofitable patients use with alarming consistency

1. "Money is definitely an issue."
2. "I don't think I can explain this in only five minutes."
3. "I already saw the people in my free community health clinic, and I didn't feel like I got enough personalized interaction there."
4. "I've already seen several other doctors, so I'm hesitant to spend more money to see you."
5. "I haven't been able to work in over a year."
6. "I have special circumstances."
7. "But I can see someone on my insurance plan for only $40."
8. "I need *help* [in a vague sense]."
9. "What professional courtesy discounts can you offer me?"
10. "I'm retired and am on a fixed income."

It's not that patients don't all have special circumstances—they do! It's just that the unprofitable patients seem to want to point their special circumstances out so you will feel sorry for them and hopefully charge less. They're also very foggy about what they need from you as a clinician.

By contrast, profitable patients will explain their circumstances, and they need a *specific result because of the special circumstances*. They have an identifiable endpoint that they seek. They have a problem, and they want a specific result.

Executives, attorneys, professionals, entrepreneurs, and other habitually busy people are accustomed to giving very specific directions, high-level summaries detailing their needs to get results. These are the patients I prefer to see.

Do not be confused into thinking that I want to see them because they have money. The real reason is that they are creatures of efficiency. To them, time is money, and they don't waste it —not theirs, not mine. No wasted time equals higher profit.

People with too much time on their hands will waste their time and yours. This is key when you're trying to identify unprofitable patients on the phone. Ambiguous goals, vague complaints, and/or a sense of confusion about their own expectations help identify them before I have to see them.

Fortunately, a patient is not my patient until I actually go to see them or render medical advice. Once I see them (or render advice), I am obligated to take care of them. They're very difficult to remove from my practice once I have established the patient/physician relationship. It is critical to avoid the time wasters before I'm stuck with them.

Occasionally, however, one will slip through the cracks.

When I find myself stuck with a "time vampire," I have to take steps to protect my own time. The way that I now identify a time vampire who is going to get me on the phone and leave long, rambling explanations without any clear goals or direction is pretty simple. If my phone rings and I see the patient's name on the phone, and I hear myself say aloud, "Ohhh Boy," I know it is time to take evasive action.

My first defense is to put strict time limits on our conversations. Anything that they cannot explain and resolve within five minutes warrants a follow-up visit at a normal house-call charge. If they hesitate, I offer them the option of a remote consultation via email or Skype at a slightly reduced rate. But they still have to pay if they want any significant chunk of my time (i.e., more than a couple of minutes. And, yes, 10 to 15 is more than a couple).

Remote consultations are also based upon time. They can have several levels ranging from a short call at $35 to an hour-long Skype session for $225. The price-tiered, time-dependent options further reinforce the concept that they need to be efficient, or they will pay for their own inefficiency.

For the patients who repeatedly seem to be disrespectful of my time, who continue to call and ask long, poorly focused questions, I use my second defense: I set my phone to send their phone calls directly to voicemail. The phone doesn't even ring when they call. They have to leave a message, which forces them to think about their issue more carefully. If they don't leave a message, I never even know that they called. This way, I don't get interrupted and distracted wondering what it is that they want.

I have found that, most of the time, these patients will self-correct quickly. If they leave a voice message that has no clear question or no clear end point, I call them back and tell them they have five minutes to ask and explain a question, and I'll help them as best I can; otherwise, they need to schedule a house call. I also apply this technique to what I consider the "three-strikes rule." Any patient that calls me more than three times with a vague question gets sent directly to voicemail.

You may think that this is harsh. You also may think that simply taking calls from these patients does not waste that much time. Granted, there are very, very few patients who fall into this category. However, I realized fairly quickly that there was a very small number of patients who were occupying the majority of my thoughts during the day. I believe that I'm compassionate, and I like to think that I'm empathetic. When a patient has a long list of problems, I instinctively want to solve them. So when these patients have an extraordinary list of problems, most of which have nothing to do with podiatry, I find my brain cannot let go of them easily. More productive thoughts are derailed.

Self-defense is the order of the day.

The value of the missed call with no message

Whenever I am seeing a patient, I turn off the ringer on my cell phone. I usually do this in front of the patient, when I sit down in their living room. I explain to them that I am turning off the ringer so that I can provide full attention to them for the entire course of their visit.

Most of the time, these patients will say, "Please feel free to get it if it's an emergency."

I then elaborate, "There is no emergency that can't wait until we've solved your problem today." This reassures the patient that I am fully attentive to their needs. This also further reinforces the discussion that we had on our initial telephone call when I explained that my practice model is based on more significant patient/physician interactions. They need to know that I am interested in their problem and will not be distracted.

During virtually every visit that I have with the patient, the cell phone vibrates. I, of course, ignore it. I just have a brief thought in the back of my mind that says, "There is another patient that I will get to see in the next day or two."

Once in a while, the patient whom I am talking to will notice the vibrating cell phone. "You can feel free to get that, if you need to," she will say.

I explain, "Absolutely not! I'll check it as soon as were done. I'll return calls to patients the entire time I'm driving to my next appointment. So if you need to reach me, and you don't get me right away, you can be assured that I'll get to you as soon as I'm done with that particular patient, as long as you leave a voicemail." This further reinforces my attentiveness to them as a current patient. It also lets them know that they should expect to leave a voicemail that I will return within a reasonable period of time.

However, there are occasions when my phone will vibrate persistently, sometimes every few minutes. This is most often a sign of a patient that I don't want to see. Time vampires want to "catch me" so that they can engage in meandering musings that only slightly resemble actual questions. So they call again and again, never leaving a voicemail, but instead thinking I eventually will pick up.

Once I get in the car and check my messages, I look at the recent call history. I look for any phone number that appears more than once (indicating repeated calls) with no corresponding voicemail. If discovered, I add that phone number to my contacts. I have one particular contact list that I have labeled "Time Vampires." I add this number to the "Time Vampire" list. Any call coming in that has been labelled "Time Vampire" is sent directly to voicemail, without even causing the phone to ring.

How to slay a time vampire

If you see enough patients, sooner or later, you accidentally will take on a time vampire. I had one time vampire lurking in the shadows of my mind for more than three months before I truly realized how intrusive our interactions were. Until that realization, I just thought of her as "needy." My moment of clarity came as I was sitting by the pool in Hawaii. Although I had told her that I would be unavailable because I was going to be on vacation, I was answering the fourth email of the day from her. This was not my fourth email I while I was in Hawaii. It was my fourth email *of the day* from her, while I was in Hawaii. The worst part about this realization was the painful acknowledgment that I had created this situation. It was actually my fault.

It all started innocently enough. I remember in our first visit when she was explaining that she could not afford a follow-up visit because she was a student traveling from overseas. "No problem," I said, "You can just send me a quick email if you have any follow-up questions."

Little did I know that the floodgates would open. As of this writing, I have 221 emails that were sent either by her to me, or that I sent in response to her questions. That is not a typo: 221 (*two hundred twenty one*) emails! Most of these emails were incredibly convoluted, lengthy, stream-of-consciousness discussions about potential worries. There were no simple "yes or no" type inquiries.

In retrospect, the sheer volume of attention required to attend to all of these inquiries is astonishing. The fact that I was responding to her when I was on vacation makes it clear that I had set up unreasonable expectations. I also very poorly reinforced my own boundaries.

Eventually, I had to seek a resolution to this problem. She had become a full-time headache.

It is my understanding that normal varieties of vampires can be thwarted with garlic, a silver cross, or a wooden stake through the heart. While I have been tempted, I have not yet tested any of these weapons on time vampires. However, I have discovered that time vampires do recoil in horror and retreat to the shadows whenever exposed to certain types of repellents:

- Direct questions
- Strict time limits
- Charges for "email follow-up consultations"

Take the example of the very real time vampire described above. As an academic exercise, let's imagine that, instead of offering free email consultations, I respected my own boundaries and adhered to my own pricing rules. I could have charged $35 as a flat rate for each email. Had I done so for those 221 emails (including 110 responses), I would have received $3,850. Of course, she wouldn't have chosen this option—but I wouldn't have found myself sitting by the pool in Hawaii responding to her fourth email of the day, either.

Because I inadvertently had created the situation myself by not explaining up front that she was going to be charged for email responses, I did not feel it was appropriate to start charging fees after we had been corresponding via email for long periods time. So I had to find another solution.

I began by creating a special folder in my email inbox labeled "Time Vampires." Any email that was sent by this patient was electronically tagged and directed automatically to skip my inbox and land in the time-vampire coffin.

This helped a great deal. I was no longer noticing her emails on my phone. I was not tempted to return them while I was driving from one appointment to the next. I disciplined myself to checked the Time Vampire inbox and return these emails on a weekly basis. (After all, I am still professionally obligated to ensure that she isn't suffering with a condition that needs prompt treatment.)

The next action that I took was this: as soon as I noticed an email from this particular patient, I called her. As soon as she answered the phone, I said, "Hello, this is Dr. Segler. I noticed that you sent an email, but I'm driving right now, and I am in between patients, so I don't have time to read it. But I wanted to make sure you're taken care of as quickly as possible. I have approximately five minutes before I am meeting my next patient. So please quickly tell me how I can help you."

After a long pause, she said, "I don't know if I can explain it quickly. It's kind of a long story."

"Well, then, I may not be able to help you at all," I replied, "but if you would like to try, I now have about four free minutes to offer. If this is too extensive to do over the telephone, perhaps we should simply schedule a follow-up appointment."

Suddenly, she was spurred into action! She quickly explained that she had a return of her prior foot pain. I made treatment recommendations. She asked me how long it would take to resolve. I answered her. I gave her very specific directions with specific timelines to follow.

When she began to ask questions about all of the vague, various "what if such-and-such happens in the future?" types of questions, I simply replied that we would deal with that if and when it occurred. "That's not a problem that we have today. I can't treat problems that you don't have, even if they are problems you might worry about."

Believe it or not, this seemed to make sense to her. With that one phone exchange, the flood of emails slowed to a trickle. I have received only two emails from her in the past four months. Both of these emails were in reference to new and different problems. I responded to both with the most appropriate response: "I am sorry to hear that you are experiencing a new problem. I would be happy to see you to provide an accurate and complete evaluation of your condition through a convenient house call. A follow-up visit is $250, and I have the following appointment times available this week. Please let me know which time will work best for you so that we can schedule an appointment."

She declined on both occasions, which is fine with me. Time limits and specific direction, with the possibility of charges incurred, seem to be a more effective repellent than bushels of garlic and a rising sun.

Chapter 7:
Email Time Savers

One of the best ways to save time is to reduce the time documenting visits and emailing patients. I use the following email templates daily. All you have to do is cut and paste and add in the patient's name, appointment time, and address.

I attach the HIPPA form and Medical History form. If the patient is elderly, I also attach the Medicare Opt-Out Agreement form. These emails answer most of the questions the patient will ask you, if you do not send a confirmation email with this information.

Once I see the patient and I have prepared their paid invoice, I send a follow-up email. I use a template for those emails, as well.

Having pre-written emails will save huge amounts of time. Answering questions before the patient thinks to ask them will same even more time.

Feel free to take my email templates, modify as you see fit, and use them.

Email template for a young, new patient who does not need x-rays

Type in the subject line: "Appointment Confirmation and Forms"

Hello,

Thank you for scheduling an appointment with Doc on the Run Podiatry Sports Medicine House Calls. We have your appointment scheduled for ---- , 2015 at --- a.m. at ---, San Francisco, CA. If there are any issues in locating your home, I will call you directly.

In the interests of time, I have attached two forms for you. If you can, please print and sign the second page of the HIPPA short form and complete the three-page Medical History form. Completing these will help save some time for you during your visit. Just keep them, and we'll review them at the appointment.

The cost of a new-patient house-call appointment and new-patient consultation is $300. Certain treatments (such as custom orthotics, injections, surgery, etc.) require additional charges which, if necessary, will be discussed at the time of treatment.

The appointment could last anywhere from 45 minutes to 1 hour, depending on your needs, condition, questions, and treatment. Please have your running shoes, casual shoes, cycling shoes, and any orthotics inserts available so we can look at them during your visit.

Payment for services is due at the time services are rendered. We accept check, cash, and all major credit cards. We will supply you with a complete Superbill (which contains all of the ICD-9 and CPT-codes your insurance carrier will need to process a claim and reimburse you for the visit). Please be aware that we have opted out of Medicare, and our services cannot be billed to Medicare.

Please let us know if you have any additional questions. You can reach me directly at (415) 308-0833.

I look forward to meeting you.
Sincerely,

Dr. Christopher Segler

Email template for a Medicare-age new patient who does not need x-rays

Type in the subject line: "Appointment Confirmation and Forms"

Hello,

Thank you for scheduling an appointment with Doc On the Run Podiatry House Calls. We have your appointment scheduled for ---- , 2015 at --- a.m. at ---, San Francisco, CA. If there are any issues in locating your home, I will call you directly.

In the interests of time, I have attached three forms for you. If you can, please print and sign the second page of the HIPPA short form, and complete the three-page Medical History form and Medicare Opt-Out Agreement. Completing these will help save some time for you during your visit. Just keep them, and we'll review them at the appointment.

The cost of a new-patient house-call appointment and new-patient consultation is $300. Certain treatments (such as custom orthotics, injections, surgery, etc.) require additional charges, which, if necessary, will be discussed at the time of treatment.

The appointment could last anywhere from 45 minutes to 2 hours, depending on your needs, condition, questions, and treatment. Please have your running shoes, casual shoes, cycling shoes, and any orthotics inserts available so we can look at them during your visit.

Payment for services is due at the time services are rendered. We accept check, cash, and all major credit cards. We will supply you with a complete Superbill (which contains all of the ICD-9 and CPT-codes your insurance carrier will need to process a claim and reimburse you for the visit). Please be aware that we have opted out of Medicare, and our services cannot be billed to Medicare.

Please let us know if you have any additional questions. You can reach me directly at (415) 308-0833.

I look forward to meeting you.
Sincerely,

Dr. Christopher Segler

Email template for a new patient who does need x-rays

Type in subject line: "Appointment Confirmation, X-ray Info, and Forms"

Hello,

Thank you for scheduling an appointment with Doc On the Run Podiatry Sports Medicine House Calls. We have your appointment scheduled for ---- , 2015 at --- a.m. at ---, San Francisco, CA. If there are any issues in locating your home, I will call you directly.

I have sent your x-ray order to Radnet Medical Imaging. You do not need an appointment; you may go anytime that is convenient for you. They are open 8:30 a.m. to 4:30 p.m., Monday through Friday. Radnet is located at:

3440 California St.
San Francisco, CA
94118-1837 (415) 922-6767

You can find directions to Radnet here.

Make sure they give the x-ray films to you so we can look at them together.

In the interests of time, I have attached two forms for you. If you can, please print and sign the second page of the HIPPA short form and complete the three-page Medical History form. Completing these will help save some time for you during your visit. Just keep them, and we'll review them at the appointment.

The cost of a new-patient house-call appointment and new-patient consultation is $300. Certain treatments (such as custom orthotics, injections, surgery, etc.) require additional charges which, if necessary, will be discussed at the time of treatment.

The appointment could last anywhere from 45 minutes to 2 hours, depending on your needs, condition, questions, and treatment. Please have your running shoes, casual shoes, cycling shoes, and any orthotics inserts available so we can look at them during your visit.

Payment for services is due at the time services are rendered. We accept check, cash, and all major credit cards. We will supply you with a complete Superbill (which contains all of the ICD-9 and CPT-codes your insurance carrier will need to process a claim and reimburse you for the visit). Please be aware that we have opted out of Medicare, and our services cannot be billed to Medicare.

Please let us know if you have any additional questions. You can reach me directly at (415) 308-0833.

I look forward to meeting you.

Sincerely,

Dr. Christopher Segler

Email template for a laser toenail new patient

Type in the subject line: "Laser Appointment Confirmation and Forms"

Hello ,

Thank you for scheduling an appointment with Doc On the Run Podiatry House Calls. We have your appointment scheduled for ---- , 2015 at --- a.m. at ---, San Francisco, CA. If there are any issues in locating your home, I will call you directly.

In the interests of time, I also have attached two forms for you. If you can, please print and sign the second page of the HIPPA short form and complete the three-page Medical History. Completing these will help save some time for you during your visit. Just keep them, and we'll review them at the appointment.

The cost of a new-patient house-call appointment and new-patient consultation is $300. However, we will waive the house-call fee for this visit. The current discount price for the laser toenail procedure for both feet is $349. Certain treatments (such as custom orthotics, injections, surgery, etc.) require additional charges which, if necessary, will be discussed at the time of treatment. I expect that your total will be only $349.

The appointment could last anywhere from 45 minutes to 1 hour, depending on your needs, condition, questions. and treatment. Payment for services is due at the time services are rendered. We accept check, cash, and all major credit cards. We will supply you with a complete Superbill (which contains all of the ICD-9 and CPT-codes your insurance carrier will need to process a claim and reimburse you for the visit). Please be aware that we have opted out of Medicare, and our services cannot be billed to Medicare.

Also, it is important to start killing the live fungus and fungal spores in your shoes as soon as possible. You can use Clean Sweep disinfectant spray, which I will have available. The Steri- Shoe is a great alternative that uses ultraviolet light instead of chemicals. If you decide to get the Steri-Shoe ultraviolet sanitizer (to start reducing the fungal spores in your shoes as soon as possible), here is a link to order it at a discount.

If you have noticed any athlete's foot or peeling skin on the feet/toes, you also should stop by your pharmacy and buy some topical Lamisil cream. Apply the Lamisil to any peeling areas of your feet twice a day to begin treating the fungal infection in the skin. This also will help ensure success with the laser treatment.

Please let us know if you have any additional questions. You can reach me directly at (415) 308-0833.

I look forward to meeting you.

Sincerely,

Dr. Christopher Segler

Email template to send as a follow-up after a new patient visit

Type in subject line: "Your Paid Invoice is Attached"

Hello,

It was really great seeing you yesterday. I have attached a copy of your paid invoice. If you feel our time together was helpful, a brief review on Yelp! would be greatly appreciated. Or, if you are just too busy to post a review, you could Like us on Facebook in an instant! Thanks for choosing me as your foot doctor!

Sincerely,

Dr. Christopher Segler

Chapter 8:
Top Ten Essential Forms

Just as email templates can save time, forms and templates for paid invoices can save an enormous amount of time. The following forms are the ones I use most frequently in my practice. Feel free to change the name and logo and use as you need.

These are the four most important forms in your house-calls practice:

1. New Patient Clinical Form
The encounter form allows me to quickly document the visit completely.

2. Medical History Form
The medical history form is extremely useful in that it can be sent to the patient prior to the house call. When they complete this form, they essentially have provided you with a written record of the subjective portion of your note. This will dramatically cut down the amount of time you spend documenting your interaction after the visit.

3. HIPPA Form
HIPPA laws are real laws with real penalties for those who fail to comply. In order to make sure that I am HIPPA compliant, I provide a copy of the HIPPA policy to every patient at their first visit. I also have them print and sign an acknowledgment of receipt of the policy.

4. Medicare Opt-Out Agreement
The Medicare opt out agreement is sent to any patient who has Medicare. This is a legal requirement. If you have opted out of Medicare, you are required to inform the patient that your services will not be billed to Medicare and cannot be billed to Medicare by either party.

Although these four forms are critical, there are many others that will simplify your practice. I have included six additional forms for you to view and use:

5. About Our Doctor Form

6. Letterhead

7. Contrast Bath Instructions

8. Orthotics Brochure

9. Laser Toenail Brochure

10. Invoice/Superbill Templates

1. New Patient Clinical Form

This form will be your clinical note. You will also use it to record the intake patient demographic information such as name, phone number, email, and address. You will begin creating the chart for the patient with this form as the moment the patient calls you. Here's how it works:

My cell phone rings, and I answer the phone, "Doc The Run—this is Doctor Segler."

"You mean, I'm actually talking to the doctor?" the patient says in a mildly surprised yet confused tone.

"Well, certainly," I respond. "Didn't you call a doctor?"

She laughs. "Why, yes, but I didn't think that I'd get to speak with a real doctor!"

I respond, "I think you ought to get to speak to a doctor—if you call a doctor, that is."

"Well, in that case, my name is Amanda, and I've been having pain in my Achilles for the past week or two whenever I run."

I grab a blank, pre-assembled, New-Patient Folder from the rack on the left side of my desk. I begin writing down everything the patient says. I also look at the caller I.D. on my cell phone and write down her phone number on the form, as well. I write "Amanda" on the top line of the form. As she explains her injury, I take down all relevant information.

Patient Name: Amanda Jones_____DOB: 12/14/1967_____
Address: 236 Main St., Yourtown, CA 94110_____
_____
Phone #:   555-867-5309_____Email: amandajones@gmail.com
Chief Complaint: Pain in my Achilles for the past week or two whenever I run

By the time Amanda finishes explaining what has been going on with her Achilles tendon, I have recorded her name, phone number, and most of the pertinent clinical information regarding her condition. Of course, I explain that I can help her and would be happy to see her during a house call. I ask her for her home address and email address and enter those on the form, as well.

Once I get to the patient's home, I use this clinical form to record her entire patient visit. The form has most of the relevant clinical information that can be circled or entered by checking the appropriate box. There is also an area for recording written notations under each section.

This serves as the primary patient record. With this form, the documentation of the patient visit can be completed in only five or ten minutes. Because this form will be placed in the chart and viewed only by me, I use relatively inexpensive paper: "Office Depot Premium

Multipurpose Bright White Paper," Letter 8.5" x 11", 20 lb., 96 Brightness, 500 Sheets. This paper is available at Office Depot and amazon.com.

New Patient Clinical Form - page 1

New patient Clinical Form - page 2

New Patient Clinical Form - page 3

New Patient Clinical Form - page 4

2. Medical History Form

The Medical History Form will be used to record the past medical history to complement your clinical note. This form will be emailed to the patient in advance of the house-call visit.

When you arrive at the house, you will ask, "Did you receive all of the paperwork that I sent to you?"

The patient will respond, "Oh, yes. Here it is," as she hands the completed new patient paperwork to you.

One of the forms that she will hand you will be the Medical History Form. It will include the patient's name, date, age, date of birth, height, weight, shoe size, and all the NLDOCAT components of the history of present illness. All other pertinent medical history, including allergies, chronic medical issues, medications, prior hospitalizations, and surgeries also will be included on the form. The social work history family history and complete review of systems will also have been completed by the patient.

As you sit in the patient's home and review the completed forms with the patient, you can discuss any pertinent findings as they relate to the patient's present medical condition.

Have the patient complete all of the past medical history and specifics of the history of the present illness prior to your arrival at the patient's home. This will substantially reduce the amount of time involved in the patient interview. It also will decrease the amount of time you must dedicate to documenting the clinical visit as a component of the medical record.

If the form has been filled out, and this information has been completed, you can simply check the boxes on the top of page 1 of the New Patient Clinical Form, which read:

Subjective: ☐ See Medical History or initial encounter form for subjective NLDOCAT ☐ Reviewed no changes

By sending an email to the patient with this form as an attachment and then checking the two boxes shown above, you will have completed all the past medical history in only a few seconds.

This form will be kept in the patient chart as a part of the patient record. Because this form will be placed in the chart and viewed only by me, I use relatively inexpensive paper: "Office Depot Premium Multipurpose Bright White Paper," Letter 8.5" x 11", 20 lb., 96 Brightness, 500 Sheets. This paper is available at Office Depot and Amazon.com.

Medical History Form - page 1

Doc On the Run - San Francisco Bay Area Podiatry House Calls
236 West Portal Ave., #332, San Francisco, CA 94127

Dr. Christopher Segler, DPM
415.308.0833

Medical History

Name: _____ Today's Date: _____ Age: _____

Date of Birth: _____ Height: _____ Weight: _____ shoe size: _____

How did you hear about us? _____

Chief Complaint
Why are you seeing the doctor today? _____

_____

Most of my pain is in the: (please circle one) right — left — both.

Nature of pain: (please circle) aching — throbbing — sharp — shooting — burning — electrical — radiating

Location: (circle all that apply) right — left — both — foot — ankle — leg

Duration How long have you had this problem? _____ days — months — years

How many days a week do you have pain? _____ days each week.

How many days a week does your pain limit your activities? _____ days per week.

Current pain level: (please circle one) (least pain) 0 1 2 3 4 5 6 7 8 9 10 (most pain)

Onset: (circle all that apply) came on suddenly — came on gradually — off and on

Course: (circle all that apply) getting worse — staying the same — getting better — comes and goes

Aggravation: My pain is worse when: (please circle one) I step out of bed — when active — resting - at night.

What makes it better: _____

Treatment: List any treatment, test, or X-rays you have had for this problem: _____

Current problem is the result of a(n):

_____ Car Accident _____ Work Accident _____ Other Accident _____ NOT Accident Related

_____
Date of Accident   Location (Home, School, Work, etc.)   Details of Accident or Injury

Doctor signature/reviewed with patient_____ Date: _____ 1
Christopher P. Segler, DPM

Medical History Form - page 2

Doc On the Run - San Francisco Bay Area Podiatry House Calls
236 West Portal Ave., #332, San Francisco, CA 94127

Dr. Christopher Segler, DPM
415.308.0833

Medical History

Past Medical History

Allergies: _____

List all current medical issues/problems: _____

_____
_____
_____

Current Medications

Medication	Dose	Times/Day	How Long

Prior Surgeries and Hospitalizations

Surgeries/Hospitalizations	Year	Reason

Have you ever had general anesthesia? _____ No _____ Yes

Ever had any problems with anesthesia? _____ No _____ Yes Describe: _____

Any family history of problems with anesthesia? _____ No _____ Yes Describe: _____

Ever had any problems with Novocain or dental injections? _____ No _____ Yes
Describe: _____

Doctor signature reviewed with patient_____ Date_____ 2
Christopher P. Segler, DPM

Medical History Form - page 3

Doc On the Run - San Francisco Bay Area Podiatry House Calls
236 West Portal Ave., #332, San Francisco, CA 94127

Dr. Christopher Segler, DPM
415.308.0833

Medical History

Social History

Employment

_____ Employed (occupation _____) _____ Work in the home _____ Student

Marital Status _____ Single _____ Married _____ Divorced _____ Separated _____ Widowed

Do you live alone? _____ No _____ Yes Children _____ No _____ Yes # _____

Exercise _____ Daily _____ Weekly _____ Monthly _____ Rarely _____ Never Type of exercise? _____

Diet: Are you on a special diet? _____ No _____ Yes. Describe: _____

Tobacco /Alcohol/ Drugs Usage

Do you smoke currently? _____ No _____ Yes. _____ packs/day for _____ years

Quit smoking? _____ This year _____ 1 yr ago _____ 5 yrs ago _____ 10 or more yrs ago

(Previously smoked _____ packs/day for _____ years)

Alcohol? _____ Daily _____ 1-2x/week _____ 1-2x/month _____ 1-2x/year

History of substance abuse? _____ No _____ Yes. What? _____

Family History Do any of your family members have a history of the following:

Diagnosis	Circle		Relationship to you:
Diabetes	No	Yes	_____
High Blood Pressure	No	Yes	_____
Rheumatologic disorder	No	Yes	_____
Heart Disease	No	Yes	_____
Stroke	No	Yes	_____
Bleeding Disorders	No	Yes	_____
Kidney Disease	No	Yes	_____
Mental Illness	No	Yes	_____
Cancer	No	Yes	_____

Review of Systems

Are you currently having or have you had problems with: (Please circle all that apply)

General/Constitutional: nausea—chills—vomiting—fever—night sweats—weakness—	NONE
Eyes/Ears/Nose/Throat: glasses/cataracts—hard of hearing—sinuses—difficulty swallowing	NONE
Lungs: COPD—asthma—shortness of breath—cough—TB—cannot sleep lying flat —	NONE
Heart: chest pain—heart disease—heart attack—stent/bypass surgery— high blood pressure	NONE
Gastrointestinal: stomach ulcers —reflux disease—colitis—constipation—upset stomach	NONE
Genitourinary: bladder problems—prostate problems—urinary tract infection— incontinence	NONE
Endocrine: diabetes—thyroid problems—liver trouble—kidney trouble—dialysis	NONE
Hematological: Cancer —Bleeding problems—blood thinners	NONE
Vascular: swelling in feet/legs/ankles — circulation problems to feet— high blood pressure	NONE
Neurological: numbness—tingling—electrical shooting pains in feet/ankles/legs— seizures	NONE
Dermatological: infection—open wound—redness— ingrown toenail —painful toenails— bruising— bleeding—warts—calluses—cracking heels— dry/peeling skin —sweaty feet—athlete's foot—	NONE
Musculoskeletal: heel or arch pain—ball of foot pain—top of foot pain—pain/fatigue of feet/legs/ankle —weak or unstable ankles—Achilles tendon pain—difficulty with brisk walking or running— arthritis	NONE

Description: _____

_____
_____

Doctor signature/reviewed with patient_____ Date_____ 3
Christopher P. Segler, DPM

Medical History Form - page 3

3. HIPPA Form

This form will be emailed to the patient in advance of the house call visit.

HIPPA laws require that you notify patients of any potential disclosures that may be made to any third party regarding protected health information. This form is two pages. One page will notify patients of Privacy Practices utilized by your podiatry house-calls practice. The second page will provide a signed acknowledgment of receipt of notice of privacy practices for you to retain for your records in the patient's chart.

This HIPPA form is substantially more specific than necessary. However, unless you set up a secure electronic patient communication portal, it is necessary to inform patients that there is disclosure risk in emailing or even speaking on a cell phone about health-related issues. Setting up a secure communication portal can be costly and cumbersome. Part of the benefit the patients receive when choosing a direct-care type practice such as the one that you are offering, though, is that they will have more direct access to you, the doctor. Telephone calls via cell phone and email communications are fast and cost-effective.

Given today's current communication standards, including cell phones, email, and video chat programs such as Skype, Google Hangouts on Air, and FaceTime, it is necessary to have a more comprehensive Notice of Privacy Practices. The patient should understand that it is possible a third party could hack into their email or cell phone and discover health-related communications information that normally would be protected by the physician–patient relationship confidentiality expectations. Your HIPPA form should inform them of these risks. All the above-mentioned forms of electronic communication are inherently insecure.

The HIPPA form that I have developed requires patients to specifically provide written authorization for patient–physician communication via electronic forms of communication. The patient can choose on this form which forms of electronic communication they would prefer to use to communicate with you after the house call visit. They then may decide to communicate with you via voicemail, email, Skype, or text message. If they choose to accept the risks of inherent non-secure electronic communication, they must provide their initials on the block at the left-hand side of each specific authorization. They then write the preferred email address, preferred telephone number, and so on.

This is the form that I use in my practice. I believe it is sufficient and will protect me from risk during a HIPPA audit. However, *I am not an attorney*. You should consult with a healthcare attorney to verify the legitimacy of the use of this form in your practice in your community.

Even though the form is emailed to the patient in advance of the visit, I always keep additional copies with me in the event that they were not able to print it at home. You must have this form in your patient chart! Because this form will be placed in the chart and viewed only by me, I use relatively inexpensive paper: "Office Depot Premium Multipurpose Bright

White Paper," Letter 8.5" x 11", 20 lb., 96 Brightness, 500 Sheets. This paper is available at Office Depot and Amazon.com.

HIPPA Form - page 1
Copy given to patient

HIPPA Form - page 2 Copy
bearing patient's signature
(to be kept in Patient Chart)

4. Medicare Opt-Out Agreement

The Medicare Opt-Out Agreement is critical. If you previously have accepted Medicare and then opted out (after you realized that it was very difficult to offer high-quality, caring interactions at low Medicare reimbursement rates), you must notify every Medicare-eligible patient that you have opted out of Medicare. In effect, when you see a Medicare patient after you have opted out of Medicare, you are entering into a private contract.

The following are conditions and requirements of a private contract between the physician/ practitioner (you) and the Medicare "beneficiary" (the patient):

- Put the contract in writing, in print sufficiently large to ensure that the beneficiary is able to read the contract.
- Clearly state whether the physician or practitioner is excluded from Medicare.
- State that the beneficiary or his or her legal representative accepts full responsibility for payment for the physician's or practitioner's charge for all services furnished by the physician or practitioner.
- State that the beneficiary or his or her legal representative understands that Medicare limits do not apply to what the physician or practitioner may charge for items or services furnished by the physician or practitioner.
- State that the beneficiary or his or her legal representative agrees not to submit a claim to Medicare or to ask the physician or practitioner to submit a claim to Medicare.
- State that the beneficiary or his or her legal representative understands that Medicare payment will not be made for any items or services furnished by the physician or practitioner that otherwise would have been covered by Medicare if there was no private contract and a proper Medicare claim had been submitted.
- State that the beneficiary or his or her legal representative enters into the contract with the knowledge that he or she has the right to obtain Medicare-covered items and services from physicians and practitioners who have not opted out of Medicare, and that the beneficiary is not compelled to enter into private contracts that apply to other Medicare-covered services furnished by other physicians or practitioners who have not opted out.
- State the expected or known effective date and expected or known expiration date of the opt-out period.
- State that the beneficiary or his or her legal representative understands that Medigap plans do not, and that other supplemental plans may elect not to, make payments for items and services not paid for by Medicare.
- Have the contract signed by the beneficiary or his or her legal representative and by the physician or practitioner.

Please note: You are required to have your patients sign a new contract every two years. I simply have *every Medicare patient* sign a copy *every year* whenever I see them. Check with your healthcare attorney to make sure you are in complete compliance.

Keep original copies of forms! Retained original signatures of both parties are required by the physician for the duration of the opt-out period (as in forever). These must be made available to CMS upon request. Place a copy in the patient's new patient folder at their initial visit before items or services are furnished to the beneficiary under the terms of the contract.

Because this form will be placed in the chart and viewed only by me, I use relatively inexpensive paper: "Office Depot Premium Multipurpose Bright White Paper," Letter 8.5" x 11", 20 lb., 96 Brightness, 500 Sheets. This paper is available at Office Depot and Amazon.com).

DOC ON THE RUN

DR. CHRISTOPHER SEGLER
FOOT & ANKLE SURGEON
AWARD-WINNING EXPERTISE 24/7
(415) 308-0833

MEDICARE Opt out patient agreement – Dr. Segler

This agreement is between Dr. Christopher P. Segler, DPM ("Physician"), whose principal place of business is 236 West Portal Ave., #332 San Francisco CA, 94127.,and patient _____ ("Patient"), who resides at _____(address) and is a Medicare Part B beneficiary seeking services covered under Medicare Part B pursuant to Section 4507 of the Balanced Budget Act of 1997. The Physician has informed Patient that Physician has opted out of the Medicare program effective on July 1, 2010 for a period of at least two years, and is not excluded from participating in Medicare Part B under Sections 1128, 1156, or 1892 or any other section of the Social Security Act.

Physician agrees to provide the following medical services to Patient (the "Services"):
-Medical out patient evaluation and treatment.
In exchange for the Services, the Patient agrees to make payments to Physician pursuant to the Attached Fee Schedule. Patient also agrees, understands and expressly acknowledges the following:
Patient agrees not to submit a claim (or to request that Physician submit a claim) to the Medicare program with respect to the Services, even if covered by Medicare Part B.

Patient is not currently in an emergency or urgent health care situation.

Patient acknowledges that neither Medicare's fee limitations nor any other Medicare reimbursement regulations apply to charges for the Services.

Patient acknowledges that Medi-Gap plans will not provide payment or reimbursement for the Services because payment is not made under the Medicare program, and other supplemental insurance plans may likewise deny reimbursement.

Patient acknowledges that he has a right, as a Medicare beneficiary, to obtain Medicare-covered items and services from physicians and practitioners who have not opted-out of Medicare, and that the patient is not compelled to enter into private contracts that apply to other Medicare-covered services furnished by other physicians or practitioners who have not opted-out.

Patient agrees to be responsible, whether through insurance or otherwise, to make payment in full for the Services, and acknowledges that Physician will not submit a Medicare claim for the Services and that no Medicare reimbursement will be provided.

Patient understands that Medicare payment will not be made for any items or services furnished by the physician that would have otherwise been covered by Medicare if there were no private contract and a proper Medicare claim were submitted.

Patient acknowledges that a copy of this contract has been made available to him. Patient agrees to reimburse Physician for any costs and reasonable attorneys' fees that result from violation of this Agreement by Patient or his beneficiaries.]

Executed on _____[date] by

_____[Patient signature]

and Dr. Christopher P. Segler, DPM [Physician name].
_____[Physician signature]

236 WEST PORTAL AVENUE. SUITE #332, SAN FRANCISCO, CA 94127-1423
PH: (415) 308-0833   FX: (650) 993-8574

WWW.ANKLECENTER.COM

---

5. About Our Doctor Form

"If you don't toot your own horn, don't complain if there's no music." —Guy Kawasaki.

When I first started my own practice, I believed that patients would research me thoroughly. I thought they would try to find out whether my interests were in alignment with their goals. I thought they would understand the amount of training I had undergone. I believed they would know if I had any particular area of expertise that they might find useful for their particular condition. I also assumed they would find any research that I had published and the surgical instrument that I invented and patented.

I was wrong.

One day, an elderly patient who I had been seeing for a couple of years showed up in the office wearing a surgical shoe. I asked her what had happened. She explained that she had just had bunion surgery (specifically, a Lapidus bunionectomy). A little bit stunned, I asked her if there was some particular reason why she had not asked for me to do her bunion surgery, since she already had been my patient. She explained that she had no idea that I did surgery, that I had done a three-year reconstructive podiatric surgical residency, that I had invented the instrument that many people used to perform the Lapidus procedure, that I had conducted research on outcomes after the Lapidus procedure, or that I had presented the research at the American Podiatric Medical Association meeting.

No matter how much information you have on your website, and no matter how much you think your patients may or may not research you, there is a very good chance that your patients will have little or no idea about who you are or what your skills and qualifications for providing care are. Even if a patient has researched you carefully and does know quite a bit about you, there is a good chance that the New-Patient Folder that you have given to the patient at their initial evaluation may be handed to one of their friends, coworkers, or relatives. Many times, I appear at a new patient's home and find one of the New-Patient Folders I have given to another patient sitting there on the patient's coffee table. They likely read materials in that folder and picked me.

It is important to include information that makes you appear qualified, personable, and human. If you are developing a podiatry practice that has a sports-medicine slant, you should include information about your athletic background and personal interests.

The About Our Doctor form is your chance to toot your own horn. Obviously, you don't want to be boastful, but on one sheet of paper, you can include a great deal of information that helps your patients understand you are qualified to provide high-quality care for them. It is also appropriate to explain why you have chosen the house-call model.

It is best to use high-quality, heavy, resume-type paper for the letterhead. High-quality paper does make an impression. I use Southworth 100% Cotton Business Paper, Letter 8.5" x 11", 32 lb., Ivory, 250 per Box (stock #JD18IC). This paper matches well aesthetically to the New-Patient Folder that I provide to the patient at the visit. It also matches the logo colors well. This paper is available at Office Depot and Amazon.com.

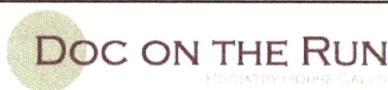

DOC ON THE RUN

About The Practice

Doc on the Run is not your average podiatry practice. Most runners have busy schedules—balancing their work and family life along with trying to find time to run. Familiar with this dilemma, Dr. Segler provides a great convenience for his athletic patients by making house call appointments. His practice has also been structured in a way that allows him to spend four to five times longer with each patient than today's average medical practitioner. This allows for the most comprehensive and informative evaluation including complicated gait exams, thorough explanations and education on a patient's particular condition, and customized treatment plans to ensure a safe rapid return to running.

Conditions and Treatments

Common runner conditions and treatments include, but are not limited to, the following:

- Shin splints
- Stress fractures
- Achilles tendon pain
- Ankle sprains
- Heel pain
- Gait analysis
- Custom running orthotics
- Custom cycling orthotics
- Platelet Rich Plasma Treatment
- Foot & ankle fracture treatment

About Dr. Segler

As a runner and triathlete himself, our San Francisco based foot & ankle surgeon has a unique perspective on foot and ankle injuries. With a keen interest in Sports Medicine, Dr. Segler lectures on running injuries and has authored a chapter in a Sports Medicine textbook. He has presented his award winning research at medical conferences in the Unites States, Canada, New Zealand and Portugal. He has completed several marathons and is a 12-time Ironman Triathlon finisher with a personal best of 10:59:07. He is currently training to qualify for the Ironman World Championships in Kona.

As an accomplished athlete himself, Dr. Segler understands how important prompt return to activity can be for a runner with foot or ankle problems. He understands that the common doctor's notion of "just stop running," "find another hobby," or "take up Scrabble" are not acceptable solutions. He believes that any athlete can suffer an injury and still return to sport stronger than ever. His recent patients include multiple world champion triathletes, prior Olympic trials marathon runners, members of the U.S. Ski team and San Francisco Giants and professional Ironman triathletes. His sports medicine podiatry practice focuses on keeping runners out on the road.

Mailing Address
236 West Portal Ave. Suite 332
San Francisco, CA 94127
(415) 308-0833
DrSegler@AnkleCenter.com
www.AnkleCenter.com
www.DocOnTheRun.com

6. Letterhead

The letterhead is used to list the patient's conditions, enumerate treatments, and draw illustrations to help the patient better understand the cause of discomfort and the action plan.

During the patient interview and clinical visit, I draw pictures that help the patient understand their condition. I draw foot and ankle images that show the important structures. I write down all of the diagnosed conditions. I also write down all the treatment options. Once I am done making all the notes on the sheet of letterhead, I take a picture with my cell phone. This picture will be pasted into the patient's clinical note. In effect, this step has saved me from writing the "Assessment" and "Plan" portions of the patient's clinical note.

Patients seem to be very impressed with a doctor who will take the time to draw a picture of a foot to help them better understand what might be causing their aches and pains. This small step seems to make a tremendous difference in the likelihood that they will share this information with their friends and relatives.

I place this sheet of paper in the patient's New-Patient Folder, along with any related/relevant patient-education handout materials that I might have in my briefcase. For example, if a patient has plantar fasciitis, I also include the patient-education handout on plantar-fasciitis treatment. I also include a general informational piece on plantar fasciitis. Because I believe contrast baths to be more effective than icing, I include the written instruction sheet on contrast baths. I also include the patient-education piece on custom orthotics. I also include prewritten patient education pieces on ESWT and PRP injections for plantar fasciitis.

The letterhead with all of your hand-drawn illustrations and written instructions is the most likely sheet of paper in the New-Patient Folder to be shared with the patient's family and friends. It is best to use high-quality, heavy, resume-type paper for the letterhead. High-quality paper does make an impression. I use Southworth 100% Cotton Business Paper, Letter 8.5" x 11", 32 lb., Ivory, 250 per Box (stock #JD18IC). This paper matches well aesthetically to the New-Patient Folder that I provide to the patient at the visit. It also matches the logo colors well. This paper is available at Office Depot and Amazon.com.

DOC ON THE RUN

Dr. Christopher Segler
Foot & Ankle Surgeon
Award-Winning Expertise 24/7
(415) 308-0833

236 West Portal Avenue, Suite #332, San Francisco, CA 94127-1423
Ph: (415) 308-0833   Fx: (650) 993-8574

www.AnkleCenter.com

7. Contrast Bath Instructions

I recommend contrast baths instead of icing for the vast majority of musculoskeletal complaints. I frequently hear follow-up patients remarking that they had never heard of this option but find it incredibly effective. For that reason, I place this instruction sheet in every New-Patient Folder. When I do see a patient where it would be inappropriate, I simply remove this sheet of paper from the New-Patient Folder (for example, a patient who is having laser toenail fungus removal obviously does not need to know about the contrast baths).

I prefer the feel of smooth paper to glossy for pieces the patient may refer to repeatedly. For the Contrast Bath Instructions, I use "Hammermill Color Copy Paper," 100 Brightness, Legal 11" x 17", 28 lb., 500 Sheets (stock #102541). This paper is available from at Office Depot and Amazon.com.

DOC ON THE RUN

DR. CHRISTOPHER SEGLER
FOOT & ANKLE SURGEON
AWARD-WINNING EXPERTISE 24/7
(415) 308-0833

Contrast Bath Instructions

Contrast baths are an effective way to reduce the inflammation associated with ankle sprains, tendonitis and other forms of acute inflammation. We recommend that you do the following once or twice a day, particularly at the end of the day or after activity. This will take about 20-30 minutes total.

Prepared two pans of water large enough to soak the foot/ankle:
- One soaking pan with cold/ice water
- One soaking pan with warm/hot water

Place the foot/ankle in the **cold**/ice water for 3-5minutes
Take the foot out and immediately place in warm/**hot** water for 2-3minutes
Take the foot out and immediately place in **cold**/ice water for 2-3minutes
Take the foot out and immediately place in warm/**hot** water for 2-3minutes
Take the foot out and immediately place in **cold**/ice water for 3-5 minutes

* ALWAYS start and end with the cold/ice water.

Do not do this if you have diabetes or peripheral arterial disease.
Call ***Doc On The Run Podiatry House Calls*** at 415-308-0833 to talk directly with Dr. Segler anytime you have questions or concerns.

Take care of yourself and get better fast!

Sincerely,

Dr. Christopher Segler
Award Winning Podiatrist
San Francisco Bay Area
Available and On-call 24/7

Warning: DO NOT perform contrast baths if you have any history of diabetes, peripheral vascular disease, poor blood flow, frostbite or Raynaud's. **Never begin any treatment without your doctor's advice.**

236 WEST PORTAL AVENUE, SUITE #332, SAN FRANCISCO, CA 94127-1423
PH: (415) 308-0833   FX: (877) 800-1825

WWW.ANKLECENTER.COM

8. Orthotics Brochure

There are three reasons why it is necessary to include the Orthotic Brochure in every New-Patient Folder:

- Custom orthotics are useful and helpful for the vast majority of patients.
- Custom orthotics are low risk and relatively profitable.
- Your patient may hear someone mention a need for custom orthotics. You want your patient to be able to recommend you as a provider in that conversation.

You should modify the Orthotics Brochure to best fit your ideal practice. I specialize in treating running injuries. For that reason, the vast majority of my custom Orthotics Brochure is designed to speak to the worldview of an endurance runner who might be suffering from foot pain. If your target audience consists of runners, great! Simply modify this form by changing the name and address on the form, and you're ready to go.

However, if you do not want to see runners, you should modify your Orthotics Brochure to target the specific concerns of your chosen patient population. You want to narrow the focus of your brochure in order to specifically speak to the patients whom you prefer to see in your practice. For example, if you specialize in diabetic patients, you might want to include more information that is relevant to the prevention of diabetic foot ulcerations. If you see many older patients, you might want to discuss the implications of custom orthotics in treating metatarsalagia and rheumatoid arthritis.

Either way, the goal is to make sure that you are offering a service that your patients can find useful. Including this brochure in the patient's New Patient Folder can help to ensure that they are aware of a valuable service that you are offering. Do not assume that your patient will assume you can make custom orthotics for them if they ever need them.

Because the Orthotics Brochure is essentially a marketing piece, it is preferable to print it on relatively high-quality paper. The images appear crisp and clean on smooth, non-glossy paper. I specifically use "Hammermill Color Laser Gloss Paper," 94 Brightness, 32 lb., Letter 8.5" x 11", 300 Sheets per Pack (stock #16311-0). This paper is available at Office Depot and Amazon.com.

PERFECT FORM

BECAUSE MOTION IS LIFE...

at Doc On The Run we offer custom solutions to help you run faster, avoid injury and alleviate running related pain.

Biomechanical Perfection

Orthotics Brochure - page 1

PERFECT FORM CUSTOM RUNNING ORTHOTICS

The Biomechanical Exam: What exactly is the problem?

The Orthotic Prescription: Your lower extremities by the numbers

Orthotic Casting: A corrected perfect impression of you

Your Custom Orthotics... Delivered

Orthotics Brochure - page 2

9. Laser Toenail Brochure

Much like the Orthotics Brochure, the Laser Toenail Brochure is an important piece to include, because many patients have toenail fungus. It is possible a patient you treat for plantar fasciitis may have a spouse or friend who mentions toenail fungus as soon as your patient mentions their visit with you. You want your patient to be aware you can treat this condition.

Don't ever assume that, just because you are a highly trained podiatrist with a broad range of treatment offerings, your patients will know it. It is not the patient's job to know what services you offer—it is your job to make sure that your patients know which services you offer. Make an effort to make them aware of the valuable (useful for the patient, high-profit for you) services.

The Laser Toenail Brochure has been written to provide a background on toenail fungus infections, treatment options, and the laser treatment of toenail fungus. It provides useful information to patients about the treatment of athlete's foot and the development of toenail fungal infections.

If the patient asks you about the Laser Toenail Brochure, concerned that you might suspect a toenail fungal infection, just explain that, no, they do not have a toenail fungus infection, but the brochure provides useful information on the prevention of this very common condition.

Because the Laser Toenail Brochure is essentially a marketing piece, it is preferable to print it on relatively high-quality paper. The images appear crisp and clean on smooth, non-glossy paper. I use "Hammermill Color Copy Paper," 100 Brightness, Legal 11" x 17", 28 lb., 500 Sheets (stock #102541). This paper is available from at Office Depot and Amazon.com.

Laser Toenail Brochure - page 1

Laser Toenail Brochure - page 2

Laser Toenail Brochure - page 3

Laser Toenail Brochure - page 4

10. Invoice/Superbill Templates

In a cash-based practice, the financial policy is simple. In fact, I include a paragraph that explains our financial policy in the confirmation email that I send to patients:

Payment for services is due at the time services are rendered. We accept check, cash, and all major credit cards. We will supply you with a complete Superbill (which contains all of the ICD-9 and CPT-codes your insurance carrier will need to process a claim and reimburse you for the visit.)   Please be aware that we have opted out of Medicare and our services cannot be billed to Medicare.

In terms of insurance claims, the only form I give to patients is the detailed paid invoice that has all of the ICD–9 codes and CPT codes. I do not give them any additional forms to help facilitate processing of the insurance claims. There are two simple reasons: 1) certain insurance carriers may have specific forms, and 2) I do not want to imply to patients in any way that I will make certain that they get paid by the insurance carrier.

If getting an insurance company to pay a claim were a simple, straightforward process, I would still accept third-party reimbursement. I certainly do not want to become responsible for battling, appealing, or arguing against insurance company denials on behalf of the patient.

Pre-formed invoice templates will dramatically reduce the amount of time you spend on invoicing after your patient encounter. Each invoice includes the patient's name, date of birth, billing address, place of service, date of service, method of payment, and the diagnosis/ICD-9 codes and corresponding procedures performed with the appropriate CPT codes. Four examples of invoice templates are included below. Here are some notes on each:

Custom Orthotics Invoice Template
You will notice that there is a casting and materials fee of $185, which has been waived. If any discount whatsoever is given to the patient, it should be enumerated on the form. I believe it is important to make sure that patients are aware of any discounts.

Laser Toenail Invoice Template
The house-call fee has been waived. The normal price of the Laser Toenail Fungus Removal procedure has been reduced and the $501 discount clearly enumerated in a red font. The mileage fee has been waived, but also clearly enumerated in a red font. Clean Sweep antiseptic spray is made available as an adjunctive item that can help reduce the risk of re-infection.

Matrixectomy Invoice Template
If the patient has bilateral procedures, I reserve the option of providing the second at no charge. This gives you an option to provide more services at lower cost. In a similar manner, if any after-hours or weekend convenient scheduling fees are provided at no additional cost,

the discount should be pointed out by listing them on the invoice and enumerating the discount in red font.

PRP Invoice Template
Because the PRP injections are relatively expensive, I often provide patients with a Thera-Band and wobble board at no charge. I also often do not charge for the house-call fee. Whenever discounted, however, I still list these no-charge items on the invoice and enumerate them in red font to clearly point out that the patient has been given a discount.

Custom Orthotics Invoice Template

Laser Toenail Invoice Template

Matrixectomy Invoice Template

PRP Invoice Template

Chapter 9:
Last-Minute Advice

Ten important thoughts to keep in mind as you start your house-calls practice:

1. **You must decide what you want. Exactly. Clearly. Picture an image of your ideal life.**
   Be specific in your goals. Decide how many days, how much money, and which types of patients you want. If you aren't achieving your goals, it probably is because they are poorly defined.

2. **Realize that you really can have your practice exactly as you wish.**
   I don't do anything I don't want to do today. Really and truly. Design the life you want.

3. **Focus on treating the conditions you enjoy.**
   It is always more fun to do the things you do well. Focus on the skills you enjoy using.

4. **Attract patients who will be enjoyable.**

5. **Avoid negative time wasters like the plague.**

6. **Experiment with your own practice model.**
   Track the patients you like, and where they come from. Do more stuff that attracts them.

7. **Raise your fee schedule every time your schedule fills.**
   If I get stressed trying to fit everyone in, it's time to raise my prices. I've never lowered them.

8. **Be thrilled when a patient says your fees are too high.**
   The goal is 15% percent price resistance. If no one objects to your fees, they are too low.

9. **If your friends, family, and colleagues think you're crazy, you probably are on the right track.**

10. **If your life (and house-calls-based practice) isn't wonderful, blissful, fulfilling, and exciting, you are doing it wrong!**

Wishing You All The Best!

Have a question that didn't get answered?
Want more info to help you succeed in your house call practice?
Email DrSegler@DocOnTheRun.com, and I'll send my latest tips directly to your inbox.

www.ingramcontent.com/pod-product-compliance
Lightning Source LLC
Chambersburg PA
CBHW042311210326
41598CB00041B/7357